Introducing Psychology

A Practical Guide

Respective authors own all copyrights not held by the publisher.

The information herein is offered for informational purposes solely and is universal as so. The presentation of the information is without a contract or any type of guarantee assurance.

The trademarks that are used are without any consent, and the publication of the trademark is without permission or backing by the trademark owner. All trademarks and brands within this book are for clarifying purposes only and are the owned by the owners themselves, not affiliated with this document.

Chapter 1: Self-Awareness

Chapter 2: Your Beliefs

Chapter 3: Acceptance

Chapter 4: Emotional Intelligence

Chapter 5: Self-Management Skills

Chapter 6: Healthy Motivation

Chapter 7: Understanding Others

Chapter 8: Improving Relationships

Chapter 9: Forgiveness

Chapter 10: The Problem with Marriage Today

Chapter 11: Issues That Can Even Threaten Happy Marriages

Chapter 12: Signs Your Marriage is in Trouble

Chapter 13: Rebuilding Your Marriage After an Affair

Chapter 14: Unexpected Ways to Improve Your Marriage

Chapter 15: Bringing Love Back into Your Marriage

Conclusion

Chapter 1: Self-Awareness

If you have ever paid attention to any self-help programs or mildly looked into the self-help world, then you have likely heard a saying that goes "The first step to fixing a problem is admitting there is one in the first place." The reason why this saying is so wildly popular is that it is completely true. If you want to solve a problem, you must first admit that there is one. When it comes to self-counseling, admitting that a problem exists often comes from developing a sense of self-awareness. Once you have become self-aware, you can recognize where the problems lie and then create solutions to help you overcome them.

What is Self-Awareness?

The first step in self-counseling is developing a sense of self-awareness. Self-awareness is the practice of developing a greater relationship with yourself so that you can recognize various elements of your personality and traits that you may carry. A person who has built their self-awareness would be far more likely to identify what types of things cause them to feel a certain emotion, the reason why the emotion exists in the first place, and the typical ways that they respond to those emotions. For example, they may know that when someone calls them a certain nickname, they get angry, and they would recognize that the anger stems from a childhood experience with a bully using that particular nickname. They would also recognize that their instinct reaction is to say something hurtful toward the other person and storm off in a rage. Therefore, they would be able to intentionally choose a different response that would be considered to be a more mature reaction to the situation, as opposed to storming off.

How Can Self-Awareness Help Me?

Self-awareness is the key tool in discovering who you are, why you are who you are, and what types of triggers and instinctual reactions you have in life. We all have them, so it is important that you first realize that you are not a unique individual who is free of triggers and emotional reactions. They are a part of human nature, and they are something that we must all learn to live with.

To shed a more positive light on self-awareness, do not consider it as a tool that shows you everything that is wrong with you. Instead, consider it a keyhole that gives you some insight into who you are and provides you with the basis for what types of changes you need to make to successfully live the life you desire to. In other words, this is not a dreadful look into your faults, but rather a positive peep into what you have the power to improve on and how you can transform your life for the better.

How Can I Develop My Self-Awareness?

You may have already noticed areas in your life where you need improvement. This awareness is exactly the type of self-awareness that we are talking about: the ability to recognize your behaviors and actions and understand how they affect yourself and others. The fact that you are self-aware enough to recognize that you need to further explore how you can lead a more positive life and what you can do to help yourself through hardship proves that you already have some degree of self-awareness within you. Now, you simply need to expand on it. In addition to recognizing that there is a problem that should be solved, you can also begin to recognize the exact parameters of the problem and what specifically needs to be healed and altered for you to live your best life. The following solutions are wonderful practices you can use to build your self-awareness and begin noticing which areas of your life are currently being negatively impacted by your pains, traumas, and hardships.

Meditation

Although meditation may seem like a somewhat spiritual and irrelevant practice to self-counseling, it is actually a powerful tool when it comes to generating self-awareness. Furthermore, many psychologists and psychiatrists are beginning to recognize and admit to the benefits of meditation, and advise their patients to begin using this practice in their healing journeys. There is much that can be learned from meditation, so it is a great idea to begin incorporating this practice into your daily routine. Not only will it help you relax and destress from difficult and painful experiences, but it will also help you generate a sense of self-awareness that can help you move forward through your healing journey.

When you are meditating with the specific intention to generate a greater sense of self-awareness, there are some questions or thoughts that you can explore during the meditation process. Which ones you ask will depend on what point in your day you are meditating during. Choose the one that is relevant to your practice and explore the questions that follow it.

If You Are Meditating to De-stress from Something...

1. How am I feeling, exactly?
2. Where do I feel these feelings?
3. What made me feel this way? Why?
4. How did I react to this experience?
5. How would I like to react to this experience in the future?
6. What can I do to release these emotions, now, in a positive way?

If You Are Meditating for Self-Awareness...

1. What do I want to achieve with self-awareness?
2. What am I already trying that works?
3. What types of behaviors are slowing me down from my goal?
4. What changes can I implement to see greater success in my practice?

Answering these questions will help you explore what it is that you are trying to achieve, what you have done to get you to where you are, and what you may be able to do in the future to help get you to where you want to go. Take your time and do not expect it all to come up at once. If you cannot pinpoint your exact emotions, goals, and strategies, in the beginning, do not stress yourself out over this fact. Simply pinpoint what you can and expand from there. The more you practice, the better you will get.

If you really do not like meditation, you might consider asking yourself these questions while performing meditative tasks. For some people, this is as effective as meditating. Tasks like this might include things such as washing the dishes, painting, sweeping or mopping the floors, or performing other mundane and mindless tasks.

Journaling

Journaling is a powerful practice you can use to log how you are feeling, get it off of your chest, and watch your growth as you continue practicing the art of self-awareness. If you want to start journaling for self-awareness, pick a journal and set the intention that you will write in it at least once a day. Then, once each day, preferably toward the end of the day, begin writing in your journal. Write down how you felt that day, anything you may have experienced as a result of your traumas, hardships, or pain, and what your reactions to these experiences were. Do not sugar coat your journal. Instead, write everything down exactly as it happened and exactly how you felt before, during, and after the experience. The idea is to get as clear and honest as you can. Over time, as you intentionally implement change and new practices, you will see that your reactions to various triggers changes. Keeping a journal is a great way to log that.

When you are keeping a journal, do not feel pressured to write out several pages each time you put in an entry. Write as much or as little as you feel like writing while still staying as detailed as possible. If you can, write it out full hand. If you don't want to, write it in bullet-point form. If you find it is hard for you to be consistent with your writing, consider keeping your journal somewhere easy to access and set a reminder in your phone or in your calendar to write at least once per day. The more you commit and practice this, the easier it will be to remember. Furthermore, the more you write about your feelings, the easier it will be to understand and explore them. At first, it may feel awkward and uncomfortable, but soon you will be able to write freely about what you are experiencing.

Confide in Someone You Trust

It is not always easy to do everything on our own. If you are in the process of developing self-awareness, you might want to get someone involved who you can trust. This may be a close friend, family member, member of your church, or even a counselor. Speaking with someone you trust about certain experiences can be a great way to get insight on how your natural reactions and responses to various things are, and what you would like for them to be.

It is important to make sure that you truly trust the person you are confiding in and that they are clear upon the reasons about why you are confiding in them. You do not want to confide in anyone who will pity you or try and solve your problems. Instead, look for someone who will listen to you without judging you, have empathy for you, and hold space for you to explore your thoughts out loud. You may ask them for advice, but they should not be leaping into "fix it" mode without first being asked for advice by you. It is important that they act as more of a sounding board who can lead you to think and explore on a deeper level rather than as someone who will try and walk you through step-by-step what you need to do to rectify your situation.

When you talk to people, it gives you the opportunity to say things out loud. Often, when we hear our thoughts out loud, things become a lot clearer to us. Also, when we ramble on, we tend to find ourselves getting into things that are far deeper inside. These are often topics that we didn't even know affected us, but they do. It is a great way to dig around in what has caused your turmoil and get a good idea of what is making you feel so poorly and react in such a way when various things happen. You can explore why the trigger exists, how it made you feel, how you reacted, and how you would like to react or respond in the future.

Furthermore, trusted friends and family members are great for helping you recognize when you are doing things. For example, say you tend to say you are feeling okay when you are not, or you lie to get out of doing things you do not want to do. Having a trusted friend or family member who can (gently) confront you on these matters when they take place is a great way to get "caught in the act." When someone else points something out, you are far more likely to begin to take notice of it over time. Having someone you trust who will politely point out when you are engaging in the behaviors you want to cut out is a great way to begin noticing these behaviors in yourself.

Be Willing to Accept Constructive Criticism

Whether you are seeking the help of someone you trust, or if you are simply looking to ask people who can help you along the path, do not be afraid to receive constructive criticism. Some of the criticism you receive may be unwelcomed, as people often tend to give you advice that you did not ask for. In these cases, you should be willing to assert your boundaries, but you can also take what they said into consideration if you feel it is relevant or true for you.

When people offer constructive criticism, do not be afraid to listen. We often tend to immediately tune out when we hear criticism coming our way because we automatically assume it will be harsh or painful. However, not all criticism is designed this way, and in many instances, criticism is a powerful tool that can help us recognize what we need to improve on in our lives. If you are receiving welcomed criticism, intentionally come out of a place of defensiveness and listen to what the other person has to say.

A great place to begin receiving constructive criticism is actually at work. You may ask your boss what they like about your work ethic and where they would like to see improvement. Then, without getting defensive, listen to them and their answers. Take that with you and honestly begin practicing doing better at these tasks. You can also ask friends, family members, and other trusted sources who interact with you on a regular basis. Doing so can help you get an outsiders opinion on how you approach things in your life, which can make it easier for you to begin practicing awareness on these things.

Once you have begun practicing self-awareness on what others have pointed out, it will become easier to dig even deeper and become self-aware of other things, too. Focusing on what others have pointed out will eventually lead you to other realizations within yourself, and you will slowly go deeper and deeper into self-awareness as you recognize more and more of what makes you who you are.

Chapter 2: Your Beliefs

A large part of what makes you who you are is your system of beliefs. The beliefs you have about who you should be, who others should be, how things should be done, how life should be lived, and virtually everything else in your life shape who you are. When we develop a system of beliefs, we often try and fit our life into these belief systems. This can distort our perception of reality, cause us to struggle to conform to who we believe we should be, and cause us to pick up unnecessary stress when others and life itself does not conform to our belief system. Your belief system plays a large role in who you are and how you live your life. Naturally, addressing this system and giving it a much-needed update can help you begin living a better life. Let's explore how.

Where Do Beliefs Come from?

Our beliefs come from a variety of areas in our lives. In the majority of instances, beliefs we have that we have never questioned are rarely ours, to begin with. Instead, they are beliefs we have borrowed from other people. We often borrow beliefs from our parents, families, religions, cultures, government, friends, teachers, guidance counselors, other key players in our society, and society itself. Essentially, anyone who isn't us that we interact with on one level or another can offload their beliefs onto us, even if we don't necessarily believe them ourselves.

Our earliest and often deepest beliefs stem way back to our childhoods. These beliefs are instilled upon us from our parents, then our family members, then our friends, then influential leaders in our childhood, such as teachers, religious leaders, coaches, friend's parents, and other prominent authority figures. They generally include things such as:

- "I am not going to be successful in life if I don't get an education."
- "I am not attractive because I do not look like __________."
- "If I do not behave in this way, people will not like me."
- "I am not lovable because ________."
- "I deserve to be in this pain because once I misbehaved by doing ______."
- "I am a bad person if I question my religious beliefs/go against my culture/go against my family's chosen religion."

As you can see, they are often negative and cause us to push ourselves into painful contortions to try and fit into what we believe is an acceptable form of life. In fact, we often believe it is the *only* acceptable form of life and living. As a result of these belief structures, we tend to develop the idea that if we behave in any other way other than those outlined by our beliefs, we are not going to be safe, protected, loved, welcomed, or accepted. We have often developed ideas that we will in one way or another be lead to even greater pain than we are already in if we defy these beliefs in favor of something more nurturing and loving.

The beliefs we develop are not always ones we are specifically told to have. For example, we may have a belief that we must have an expensive education and an Ivy League degree to be considered successful because that is what our parents told us when we were growing up. For this type of belief, we were specifically told to believe it. However, we may also then believe that anyone who does not acquire this type of education is a failure and is then unacceptable and unlovable. This would be a belief we have based on how we interpreted what our parents told us, and not based on what they specifically said.

In many instances, these beliefs we generate based on interpretations are not accurately reflected by the beliefs of the people who originally planted these ideas in our head. For example, although your parents might not be pleased at first, if you were to drop out of school, start a company, and find yourself running a wildly successful business, your parents would likely still see you as successful. However, because they never validated this route, you would likely see it as an incomplete or unacceptable form of success because it does not follow the specific path they lead you to believe was the only successful path. So, therefore, your belief might hold you back from your unique journey because you are afraid to follow your own path to success since you now believe it is the wrong path, despite it having the same outcome.

The beliefs we have are powerful and have a strong ability to shape who we are, how we approach life, what we deem is acceptable and unacceptable, how we view ourselves, how we view others, and many other elements of our life. To sum it up nicely: our beliefs shape absolutely everything we do, see, experience, and otherwise. They touch virtually every part of our life.

How Are My Beliefs Holding Me Back?

Any belief that you have that does not belong to you has the power to hold you back. Furthermore, any belief you have that is yours but does not serve your highest good also has the power to hold you back. If you want to have a more joyous life, you need to slow down and take some time to question your beliefs. Question where they come from, why you have them, if you actually believe them yourself, and if they serve your highest good.

If they never belonged to you in the first place and you borrowed them, *and* they are not serving your highest good, there is a good chance that your beliefs are holding you back. In general, any belief that tells you that you cannot do what you want, be who you truly are, love who you love, like what you like, believe what you want to believe, or otherwise live the life you desire to live based on free will, is a negative belief. These beliefs hold us back and prevent us from achieving anything we desire to achieve in life because they tell us that our desires are fundamentally wrong. They are damaging beliefs that have an extremely negative impact on our lives, and therefore they need to be systematically changed to allow us to nurture ourselves and begin living the lives we genuinely desire to live.

How Can I Redesign My Beliefs and My Life?

Redesigning your beliefs is not an easy practice, especially for ones that you have held for a particularly long time. In general, the older the negative belief is, the more damage it has done, and therefore the more you will have to work to eradicate it from your life. It is important, however, that you do not simply erase negative beliefs. You also need to replace them with positive new ones. In other words, you need to redesign them. By redesigning your beliefs, you restructure the "box" you need to live inside of so that it nurtures who you truly are, what you want to be in life and everything that helps you lead the life you desire.

The following practices are strategies you can use to help you redesign your existing beliefs.

Challenge Outdated Beliefs

Some beliefs never served us to begin with, and some beliefs stop serving us over time. Either way, any belief that is not serving you should be considered outdated. The best way to begin eradicating these beliefs is to challenge them. We often blindly believe our beliefs simply because they have always been there, or because at one point or another someone convinced us that they were factual and necessary for us to live the life we desire to live. Whether or not that was true, we took the belief on and began living our lives in accordance with it.

If you want to change your beliefs, you need to challenge these ones, first. Challenging them gives you the opportunity to understand where they came from, why you have them, and what they have (or haven't) done for you in your life. Challenge them by answering the following questions in your journal:

1. Where does this belief come from?
2. Why do I believe it?
3. Is there any validity to this belief?
4. How do I believe this belief has protected or helped me in my life?
5. Does it actually protect or help me? If so, is it the most effective and positive method or is there a better one I can choose that will have a greater impact?
6. How has this belief negatively impacted my life?
7. How would my life look if I did not have this belief?
8. What belief would better serve me?

Become Self-Aware of How They Affect You

As you are answering the questions from above, and as you are living your day-to-day life, begin to develop a self-awareness about how your beliefs have affected your life. You may realize that some of your beliefs are more positive and that they effectively help you in life powerfully and positively. However, you will likely also realize others are negative and that they actually do not positively serve you. While they may offer the illusion of protection or security, they are likely actually putting you directly in pain and otherwise holding you back and preventing you from living life to your fullest potential.

When you begin to realize exactly how various beliefs affect you, it becomes easier to understand how they are holding you back or helping to propel you forward. For the ones that propel you forward and positively serve you, you can express gratitude. For those that are holding you back or harming you, it is time to let go of them. By realizing how they are negatively impacting your life, it suddenly becomes a lot easier to recognize them for being negative habits and to develop a willingness to shift your beliefs for a more positive outcome.

Shift Your Perspective

Your perspective is largely what holds you back and prevents you from changing beliefs that you have in your life. When you view something with a particular perspective, it can suddenly become easier to shift how you carry certain beliefs. Often, the beliefs that are negatively impacting us are either viewed from the perspective of someone else, or from the perspective of our younger self.

When someone else's perspective fosters beliefs, it is easy to see that they do not accurately reflect our true beliefs. Furthermore, there is no guarantee that they are actually benefiting us in any way. The beliefs we carry from other people are often directly picked up by the people we value and care about deeply. For this reason, we choose to blindly take on their beliefs because we want to be accepted, loved, respected, and cared for by them. However, this can lead to us taking on beliefs that do not serve us. If you are looking at beliefs from someone else's perspective, it is time to stop and look at them from your own perspective. If this person had absolutely no say in the matter, what would you believe?

When beliefs are carried on from those that we developed in childhood, they are often outdated. As children, we are unable to protect ourselves and make decisions that will keep us alive and thriving. For that reason, we rely on the people who are in charge of caring for us (often our parents and other caregivers, like daycare providers, teachers, coaches, etc.) to help us shape our beliefs. While these may help us to be guided and raised by them, it often also results in us taking on beliefs we do not necessarily agree with. Instead, these are beliefs we keep as they shape how we must think, act, speak, and otherwise behave to be accepted by those who are caring for us. Shifting your perspective, then, comes from realizing that *you* are now your caregiver and the only person you need to appeal to to protect your wellbeing is *you*. If you were to eliminate the beliefs of those who were once responsible for your very survival, what would you believe?

Affirm New Beliefs

After you have taken the time to recognize your outdated beliefs, become self-aware of how they affected you and what new beliefs you would prefer to have, and taken the time to adjust your perspective, you should be left with a fairly clear idea of what your true beliefs are. Once you have them, however, it is time to begin enforcing them into your life and removing the other beliefs that you no longer desire to maintain.

Affirming new beliefs happens in a few ways. First, it comes from recognizing when old beliefs are playing out their outdated patterns and intentionally eliminating them. For example, imagine you are interested in taking up a new class, but it teaches something that you have long believed to be inappropriate for someone of "your type" (whether it be gender, age, religion, culture, etc.). Your instinctual reaction may be to simply overlook the idea and move on to a new option or simply skip the idea of taking any classes altogether. However, once you have developed self-awareness, you can recognize that this would be an outdated belief holding you back from embarking on an experience that you believe in and would enjoy. So, then, you can take the time to affirm your new and true beliefs by going and signing up for the class and enjoying the experience.

In addition to taking action based on your new beliefs, you can verbally affirm your new beliefs as well. Say things such as "I no longer choose to believe that _______ is true. I recognize that this is not my true belief. Instead, I choose to believe that _______ is true." Intentionally and verbally stating that you are eliminating an unwanted belief and replacing it with a more positive and healthy belief is a great way to ensure that you are affirming to yourself that old beliefs no longer serve you and you have the power and authority to choose to believe new, more positive beliefs.

Chapter 3: Acceptance

A great deal of the pain, trauma, and hardship that we face is a result of wanting to be accepted. Our desire to be accepted by those we care about, such as our family, our friends, our religion, our culture, and our society, greatly shapes how we live. This shapes how we are willing to think, believe, and behave to be accepted. It also shapes how we are willing to allow others to think, believe, and behave to consider us to be acceptable. An incredibly important part of self-counseling is acceptance.

How Does My Acceptance Impact Me?

We are often so obsessed with our need to be accepted by other people that we tend to forget about our need to accept ourselves. This can lead to you completely abandoning yourself in times of need, ultimately leading to you living a life that does not nurture you as a person.

Learning to accept yourself is a powerful shift that you can make that will drastically change everything in your life. When you realize how important it is for you to accept yourself and the number of benefits you can enjoy. As a result, it becomes increasingly apparent that your self-acceptance is far more valuable than someone else's acceptance of you, no matter how much you value them in your life.

Self-acceptance is the key to loving yourself as you are. This is the very key that gives you clear permission to be yourself, love yourself, and love your life. It stops you from struggling to fit into the often unattainable ideals of others and allows you the right to choose who you want to be, and then be that person. When you choose self-acceptance over the acceptance of others, it does not mean that you are not mindful of other people's thoughts, feelings, or beliefs. Instead, it simply means that you are not willing to let someone else's thoughts, feelings, or beliefs hold you back from living a life that you genuinely love, where you genuinely love yourself, too. There are virtually no negative side-effects to self-acceptance. While it may take some time for you, and everyone else to adjust to, you will notice that the benefits far outweigh any potential resistances you may have to overcome to attain your self-acceptance successfully.

How Can I Accept Myself?

Learning to accept yourself takes time, patience, and understanding. The very idea of accepting yourself is accepting yourself exactly as you are. You can start right away by accepting yourself as someone who struggles to accept themselves. In essence, you want to accept everything about yourself: the good, the bad, and the ugly. Remember these labels are just beliefs you have concocted in your mind as a result of your environment. The truth is, you are an authentic and completely loveable being merely because you exist on earth. The idea that you have to do anything to be deemed loveable or acceptable is completely false and highly destructive to your mental wellbeing. In addition to making the conscious decision to accept yourself as you are right now in your life, there are some other changes you can make, too. The following tips will help you accept yourself as you are.

Set The Intention

The very first step to accepting yourself is setting the intention that you will accept yourself. This practice is seemingly small and takes virtually no time at all, but it is absolutely necessary if you will successfully accept yourself as you are, for who you are. You can do so now by saying something such as: "I accept myself as I am, faults and all. I am a perfectly acceptable and loveable person, exactly as I am. Nothing and no-one can change that."

Celebrate Yourself

Often the reason we struggle to accept ourselves is that we heavily focus on our flaws. We have learned to judge ourselves based on what other people believe to be acceptable, and therefore we do not accept ourselves because in many ways we do not meet the ideals. The unfortunate reality is that you will never be fully acceptable in everyone's eyes. These judgments of you, however, do not need to become your beliefs. You do not need to uphold these to be loved and accepted by those around you.

One great way to stop obsessing over your flaws and to begin celebrating your positive elements is to celebrate yourself. Begin noticing what wonderful features you possess, and celebrate them. If you spend an entire day talking positively and lovingly, celebrate that! If you succeed in reaching a goal, celebrate it! If you respond to a negative trigger with a positive response, celebrate it! Look for any reason to celebrate yourself that you can find, and celebrate yourself to the fullest. The more you practice celebrating yourself, the more you will find to celebrate. Soon, you will be more focused on your positive features rather than your perceived flaws.

After you have learned to celebrate everything you perceived to be a positive feature of yourself, it is time to move on and start accepting and celebrating all of your perceived flaws. Everything you have recognized to be negative or fault-worthy should be celebrated, allowing you the opportunity to recognize that no one is perfect and that nothing, not even something you consider to be negative about yourself, should hold you back from openly accepting and loving yourself as you are.

Check Your Self-Talk

How we talk to ourselves is often where we get hung up on the very foundation of unacceptance. This is where we fail to accept ourselves because we tend to obsess on our flaws and repetitively - and often harshly - point them out to ourselves in our negative self-talk. We often say things like:

- "You're so stupid, how did you not know that?"
- "Why would you do that? Are you dumb?"
- "What on Earth were you thinking?"
- "That's your problem: you don't think."
- "This is why Mom didn't love you."
- "You will never be loved if you keep behaving like that."
- "You are an idiot."
- "I hate you."

The things we tell ourselves are often so harsh that we wouldn't even say them to the people we do not care about, or that we dislike. They are insensitive, unkind, and are a large part of why you might not have a positive relationship with yourself. If you want to learn to accept yourself, you need to begin replacing your negative self-talk with more accepting phrases. Try things such as:

- "I accept you."
- "Mistakes happen, you are human. I accept you as you are."
- "I love you."
- "You are still loveable."
- "This does not define you."
- "I forgive you."

Grieve Your Losses

Often, we struggle to accept ourselves because we feel as though we have failed. When we are growing up, and throughout life, we often set dreams and expectations of what we will be and who we will become. We imagine our lives, our dreams, and what we desire for ourselves and our loved ones. Naturally, we do not fulfill every dream we ever set for ourselves. In fact, we may not even achieve the ones that we felt were most important to us. This is not always our own fault. Sometimes life changes and we are not given the ability to reach our goals as we thought we would, or sometimes we stand in our own way and hold ourselves back. As a result of these losses, we feel that we have become failures and that we cannot face ourselves. It is similar to handing your parents a report card with an "F" on it, or telling your boss that you fell short of an important task at work. You never want to admit that you failed. It doesn't feel good. Likewise, it's hard to admit it to yourself.

It is important that you provide yourself with the space to grieve these losses and perceived failures. When you realize a dream has been unmet and that you are not likely going to meet it in the future, or that you no longer want to meet it and you feel bad because it used to mean so much to you, it can be painful. Bringing closure by intentionally grieving these losses properly is a powerful way to overcome the pain they carry and the self-hatred we often possess as a result. Once you have grieved them, learn to accept their loss and open up space for new growth in your life.

See Yourself from a New Perspective

Holding ourselves to extremely high standards seems to be a common thing amongst humans. As a result of our beliefs and expectations in life, we believe that we are to be someone that almost resembles that of a superhuman. We believe that we are to be able to do and be everything, and get extremely disappointed in ourselves when we realize we are not capable of meeting these expectations. As a result, we get extremely unkind and critical toward ourselves. Contrary to what we may believe, these acts of hatred are not beneficial and will not motivate us to do better, achieve more, or get further in life. Instead, they cause us to believe that we are worthless. They lead us to believe that we *cannot* do more, achieve more, or get further in life. Therefore, we don't because we have officially readjusted our beliefs to believe that we are unworthy. Since we are creatures of our beliefs, we then become less than we actually are. It is actually completely counterproductive!

Try seeing yourself from someone else's perspective. Consider someone that loves you. Someone who seems to believe that you can do no wrong. How would they feel if they knew what you were saying about yourself? How would *you* feel if you learned that *they* were saying such unkind things about *themselves?* It is likely that the same way you would feel about them doing it is how they would feel about you doing it. They would likely be unhappy, and sad that you are feeling so angry at yourself. Furthermore, from the outside, they get to see all that you do accomplish: all that you often overlook from your own perspective. They get to see what you have achieved in life and the magic that you have created. If you need help accepting yourself, step outside of your own reality and imagine that you are looking in. How different does your life look from the outside?

Chapter 4: Emotional Intelligence

In each of the first three chapters, you were walked through important steps of learning to accept yourself, rebuild your foundation to nurture you and your desires in life, and recognize where you wish to improve upon. Now, it is time to begin learning how you can embrace emotional intelligence and how this very powerful skill can help you actively work toward living the life you desire to live.

What Is Emotional Intelligence?

Emotional intelligence is a skill that allows people to become aware of, control, and effectively express their emotions. This skill also enables them to handle interpersonal relationships judiciously and empathetically. What this means is that a person who is emotionally intelligent develops the ability to feel and manage their emotions in a way that is not harmful or hurtful to either themselves or anyone else. They do not bottle up their emotions, but they also do not recklessly express them in a way that is unkind or unfair towards others, or themselves.

A person who is emotionally intelligent knows how to effectively feel their emotions in a way that is productive and complete. They foster a great sense of self-awareness that enables them to recognize their emotions and to recognize what their natural emotional expressions are. They can also control themselves so that they can manage their emotions in a more productive manner that allows them to feel the emotion thoroughly, but not express it in such a way that would appear as a temper tantrum or other emotional outburst that is often seen as immature and unacceptable in social situations. For example, if an emotionally intelligent person was angered by something their boss said, rather than saying something passive aggressively or being rude to their boss, they would handle the situation logically and kindly. If necessary, they would calmly and productively explain their anger to their boss and seek to generate a resolution together that was beneficial to both them and their boss. Then, they would take the rest of the anger and use it to their benefit. For example, they may use it to fuel them to work harder or go for a run after work. Alternatively, they may express it later in a conversation with a friend, in their journal, or in another way that enables them to completely feel and release the emotion without harming anyone or anything.

How Can Emotional Intelligence Help Me?

In many cases, people with lower levels of emotional intelligence struggle to properly interpret and express their emotions in a way that is beneficial and productive. Regardless of where you presently sit on the emotional intelligence scale, working toward increasing your emotional intelligence and building your skills around this intelligence can significantly benefit you when it comes to learning how to work on your emotions effectively. This practice is essential in learning to accurately identify, articulate, and release emotions that you may encounter throughout your life.

When people lack emotional intelligence, they often struggle to recognize what is actually bothering them. They may have a general idea of what triggered their emotions, but they are likely unaware of why, or what specific emotions they are feeling. Common experiences include confusing emotions such as jealousy, envy, confusion, frustration, sadness and other similar emotions for anger. Many people who lack emotional intelligence believe they only feel about three different feelings: anger, sadness, and happiness. They do not recognize that there are hundreds of other emotions a person can experience, and they are unaware of how to recognize these emotions in themselves.

When you do not accurately identify what you are feeling emotional, it becomes infinitely harder to actually rectify the emotion. That is because you are not clear on what you are dealing with. Therefore, you are not entirely sure about what has caused it or how you might go about expressing it.

Another reason emotional intelligence is important is that it teaches you not to censor your emotions, but to control them. Rather than bottling something up and experiencing it with greater force at a later date, often exploding over something small, you learn to control how you release the emotion. This practice includes learning how to effectively deal with the emotion at the moment, what to do after the fact, and how you can go about releasing the emotion so that it no longer affects you.

How Can I Become More Emotionally Intelligent?

Developing emotional intelligence takes time and practice, but with proper personal investment you can significantly increase your emotional intelligence and learn to identify, manage, control, and express your emotions more effectively. The very first step is generating a sense of self-awareness, as this is how you will be able to recognize when you are feeling different emotions, which emotions you are feeling, why you are feeling them, and what specific feelings you are experiencing in your body as a result. If you need a refresher in self-awareness, revisit Chapter 1 before exploring the rest of the practices relating to emotional intelligence.

Learn to Identify Your Emotions Accurately

To gain emotional intelligence and complete the subsequent steps, you must first learn how to identify emotions that you are feeling accurately. Emotions often tend to cover themselves up with more basic, protective emotions like defensive or offensive anger. When we cover up our emotions, it is a natural instinct we rely on to prevent ourselves from being hurt. Often, hurt is the root cause of these emotions.

However, there are other times when emotions are covered up, too.

If you are struggling to identify your emotions, you might consider downloading and printing a mood chart. These charts are made up of tens if not hundreds of different moods you may be feeling, and they accurately explain what each mood or feeling feels like. Whenever you are feeling a certain emotion, such as anger, try and understand why you are feeling angry. You can do this by reviewing the mood chart and discovering what underlying feeling you are actually feeling. You may find that you are feeling angry because you are hurt because someone made you jealous. In a situation like this, jealousy is the real issue, and anger is a defense to prevent you from feeling jealous. Treating the anger will only treat the symptom, not the actual root cause of the problem. Before you can treat the root cause, you need to know what it is, exactly.

Understand and Change Your Natural Responses

Your natural responses are often instinctual reflexes that you call upon whenever you feel a certain emotion. For example, jumping to anger to protect yourself from pain is a natural response. While these responses have gotten you to where you are now, they are not exactly the best choice when you intend to learn how to manage your emotions more effectively. If you want to develop your emotional intelligence and begin learning how to control your emotions, rather than letting them control you, you need to call on your self-awareness and start recognizing what your responses are. Some common responses include things such as:

- Getting angry and blaming someone/hurting someone when they hurt you
- Getting extremely quiet and sweeping someone's unkind actions under the rug
- Feeling anxiety when you are being put in a situation that you know you are often hurt or mistreated in because your natural response is to let the person treat you that way (perhaps you are too afraid to defend yourself)
- Feeling jealous when people befriend your friends, or otherwise "impose" on something you have, or want
- Becoming sad when someone unintentionally hurts you (for example, forgets about an event you scheduled together, or does not call you on your birthday)

Every single person has both a trigger and a natural response to every situation. Virtually every situation you experience in life, from waking up in the morning to making coffee or cooking dinner to heading to work, everything triggers some form of emotional response from you. Even if the response is "neutral," it is still a response. Learning to identify what your natural response allows you to plan how you would prefer to respond in the future.

Once you have discovered how you respond, the next step is to discover how you would like to respond. Recognizing how you would like to respond and what response would make the situation both more effective and less painful is a great starting point. An emotionally intelligent response would be one that is polite, assertive, intentional, thought out, and beneficial or productive for everyone involved.

Then, once you have identified your intended response, you can begin to implement it. At first, it will not come easy. You will recognize yourself in the position where you should be making the better choice, and it will not happen. Soon, however, you will notice that you recognize the situation sooner and sooner and that you get better at replacing your natural response with your new, emotionally intelligent response. Then, eventually, it will be replaced altogether.

Feel and Release Emotions

In addition to responding to situations at the moment, you also need to learn to feel them and release them. Often at the moment, we do not feel our way through a feeling. Instead, it may linger and spend some time with you. Sometimes, you can address the feeling right away. You might be able to go take a short break alone and deal with your emotions by journaling, talking to a friend, or otherwise relaxing and feeling through the emotion. Other times, you may have to learn to put that emotion in your backpack and carry it with you for a little bit until you have time to be alone and deal with it. It is important that if you set the emotion aside to deal with it later, that you do return to it and deal with it later. Otherwise, you will continue to carry it with you and eventually it will come out much stronger in the future. Always face your emotions. Once you have, intentionally let them go so that you can move on.

Chapter 5: Self-Management Skills

Reading and learning new skills is not enough when it comes to self-counseling. You must take your time and learn to implement the skills, otherwise, they are simply noise clanging around in your head and making you feel worse about not seeing any positive results in your life. The best way to make the most of your new skills and see true results from them is to learn how you can manage yourself. Self-management is a skill whereby you intentionally check-in with yourself on a regular basis and see how you are doing. You should also have some form of a schedule to stick to that allows you to intentionally work on your new self-counseling skills, allowing you to invest enough time in them that you actually begin to see positive results.

What is Self-Management?

Self-management is a skill where you learn to manage yourself in every way. It is a large task to embrace, but once you learn how it becomes significantly easier.

A great way to understand self-management is to consider a business. In a business, there is a manager who is responsible for many tasks. They must schedule employees, oversee employees to make sure work is getting done, place orders for new stock, deal with any discrepancies in the business, and shoulder a lot of other responsibilities. They are essential to keeping the place running smoothly, so their position is extremely important.

Self-management is similar but in a personal sense. When you learn to self-manage, you are essentially learning to manage all of your internal operations and facilities, enabling you to function more effectively. Self-management requires self-awareness, which then allows you to manage your emotions (emotional intelligence), boundaries, beliefs, self-acceptance, self-talk, and other practices. It also works in a more practical sense, such as making effective use of time management, alone time or self-development time, and other outward skills that make your internal life significantly easier by reducing stress and having some level of attention and intention placed on all aspects of your life.

How Can I Practice Self-Management?

Self-management is a series of skills that you must learn to effectively take advantage of. The following skills are things you need to become aware of and begin practicing to maximize your self-management. These skills do not include the ones you have already learned in prior chapters.

Boundaries

Boundaries are a major part of self-management. When you have and enforce boundaries, you essentially create a system of "rules" for how you are willing to treat others and be treated by others. This allows you to have an idea of what you are okay with, and what you are not okay with. Then, when something happens that you are not okay with, it gives you the opportunity to face that and rectify it. Often, enforcing boundaries requires uncomfortable conversations with people who overstep boundaries. In some cases, the person will understand, apologize, and make a conscious effort to refrain from crossing that boundary again. In others, the person may become angered and attempt to stomp over your boundaries and bulldoze you. When people are disrespecting your boundaries, you need to have a pre-determined response that you will use to withhold your boundaries. This response is a part of your self-management, and it is necessary for helping you to respect your own boundaries and internal rule system. The best responses include completely shutting the person down, maintaining your assertiveness, and walking away. You can choose which ones you would prefer. Ideally, you should choose two: one for when you can't walk away, and one for when you can. Know how much you are willing to take before you walk away, and then honor that and walk away when that boundary is crossed.

Time Management

Learning to manage your time is important because this enables you the opportunity to set more time for yourself intentionally. People who are dealing with a lot internally tend to overschedule and attempt to stay busy to refrain from dealing with what is going on inside. Unfortunately, this just makes it significantly worse and often results in the said person having an emotional breakdown and thus abandoning many of the things on their schedule. When we don't honor our emotions and our needs, they tend to rear an ugly head at us and force us to pay attention. Instead, schedule time to pay attention. Ideally, you should have some time scheduled every day to slow down and pay attention to your needs and feelings. The best time is at night before bed. Use this time to work on your emotions and release them effectively. Then, sit in that peaceful state of release for a while before going to bed. Making use of your time in a more effective manner such as this is the best way to ensure that you are fulfilling your essential need of self-care.

Alone Time

Alone time is a vital practice that many people overlook. Once again, this is often an attempt to run away from uncomfortable feelings that you do not like. When you are faced with alone time, you likely fill it doing tasks that keep your mind busy, such as reading, video gaming, or even walking around a store to keep busy. While these are all great things to do in your downtime, or even during some of your alone time, you should also have the type of alone time where you literally sit with yourself and pay attention to yourself. This should be time where you invest in your relationship with yourself and nurture your needs. Journal, pamper yourself, and really work on developing a relationship through self-love. Pay attention to what you need and honor those needs at this time. If you just need some peace and quiet, have that. If you need to feel through some anger or sadness you have been carrying with you, feel it through. Do what you need to do at this time, and do not be afraid to have it. It may not feel wonderful every time, but once the emotions are moved out, you will feel much better overall.

Check-Ins

Checking in with yourself is a great way to boost your emotional wellbeing and manage yourself successfully. Learning to check-in with yourself means that you regularly take time to ask yourself how you are doing and if you need anything. Asking yourself this exact question and then honoring the answer you get is a wonderful way to work through anything that you may be carrying with you. Often, we are so used to bottling emotions that we don't even notice when we are doing it. Instead, it takes us a while to realize we have been doing it. Sometimes, we wait all the way until we have an emotional meltdown. Instead, learn to ask yourself how you are doing, and then take action on your response. If you are not used to doing this, consider setting a reminder on your phone each hour saying something like "How are you?" then answer it honestly in your mind. If you feel that you need to work through emotions, have some alone time, take some extra time with your spouse or family or friends or otherwise, intentionally schedule that into your near future so that you can take care of your needs.

Chapter 6: Healthy Motivation

When we have been consumed with difficult, painful, or unhappy emotions for a long time, it can be a struggle to get yourself motivated to feel better. While at times the pain itself can be motivation to make a change, at others it may feel like a life sentence of despair and anger. As you are on the path to feeling healthier, happier, and more positive overall, you will need to learn how you can tap into some healthy motivation to help yourself feel better. This type of healthy motivation will push you to feel more inspired to make a positive change in your life and claim the happiness that you deserve.

What Does Healthy Motivation Look Like?

Healthy motivation is essentially any form of motivation that is positive and inspiring, but not harmful in any way. Some people turn to perceived motivators such as drugs, alcohol, and other addictive substances to improve their mood. These may feel as though they work in the short term, but in the long term they will only worsen the problems and create more. Instead, you need to look at healthy motivational tools like exercise, positive mantras, positive goals, and even accountability partners who will help you stay motivated. Healthy motivation is anything that inspires you to do better and lead a happier, healthier life without having any form of negative repercussions.

Healthy Motivation You Can Try Today

There are many different healthy motivators you can begin taking advantage of right away to get you in a good or at least productive mood. The following are great tools that you can begin implementing in your daily life to help keep you motivated. Some should be included as a part of your routine, whereas others can be relied upon when they are needed. You can decide which will work best for you, but ideally, you should include at least 2-3 motivators to help get you started right away.

Exercise

Many coaches, counselors, and wellness experts agree that emotion is essentially "energy in motion." It is the way we feel energies in our bodies as a result of various triggers, and the way which we choose to physically express those emotions. With that knowledge, you can choose to channel your energy-in-motion more positively and productively, instead of physically taking it out in a way that is harmful and destructive to either yourself, others, or both.

Incorporating exercise into your daily schedule is a great way to keep your energy flowing and prevent energy build up. However, you can also call on energy when you need a quick release, too. For example, if you feel a significant amount of anger coming on, you might release it by going for a walk or run, doing some jumping jacks or sit-ups, or even going to the gym to take it out with some weights. Some people who have ongoing anger or stress issues also like to join classes that are cardio-based as they get your body moving and help the unwanted energy move through you so that you can clear up space for positive energy. If you feel an onslaught of difficult emotions, or if you feel that you regularly have pent-up emotions that you struggle to release, exercise is a great way to move them through your body so that you can release them completely.

Healthy Nutrition

A healthy diet is also imperative if you want to have a more positive mood and better energy to face your day with. Sometimes when we feel stressed, angry, sad, or otherwise unhappy, it can be due to a poor diet. When we consume a diet that is not meeting our nutritional needs, we often end up lacking important nutrients that help us function well. As a result, our emotional wellbeing can suffer due to physical stressors. Moving toward eating a healthy, nutritious diet is a great way to help get your body into physical wellbeing so that you can bring up your mental wellness, too. Furthermore, it can help you feel far more energetic so that you have more mental and physical alertness to face your day with.

Accountability Partner

Doing it alone can be hard, and no one says that you have to. A great motivator can be finding an accountability partner who is willing to help keep you accountable to your goals. Sometimes, motivating yourself isn't easy. Getting someone else to help with that can be a major benefit, and can keep you accountable. Accountability partners are responsible for checking in with each other and making sure that each person is keeping up with their personal goals. Often, both partners are responsible for supporting each other, so it is a mutually beneficial partnership. Each of you will ensure that the other is sticking to their goals, and motivate each other to keep charging forward. If one partner is not feeling particularly motivated, the other will help give them words of encouragement or give them a much-needed kick in the behind to move forward. Accountability partners are great at help jolting you out of your current state and encouraging you forward into action.

When you are choosing an accountability partner, make sure you choose someone that you trust. You should also choose someone who is compassionate, as you want to be motivated not bullied into action. The person you choose to form an accountability partnership with should be someone who will keep you accountable and who will not be an enabler to your old habits. Instead, they should see how badly you want to change and use that to help fuel you to move forward when you need it, cheer you on when you experience success, and ultimately keep you accountable and moving forward. And, you can do the same for them with their goals.

Visualization

The power of visualization is undeniable. Experts across the board, from coaches and mentors to counselors, psychologists and psychiatrists, and even many neuroscientists agree that visualization has a powerful impact when it comes to rewiring your brain. The commonly accepted belief is that your subconscious does not know the difference between real life and real thought. Therefore, if you continually think and visualize positive things, you can essentially rewire your brain to have a more positive outlook on life. While you can and should incorporate positive visualization into your daily routine, you can also use this on a whim if you need a boost of motivation. You can do this by taking the time to slow down and visualize yourself getting the energy and will you need to move forward from where you are right now. Even if you invest just two minutes into this visualization, the impact can be powerful and lasting. You can visualize anything from a beam of energy washing over you, to you being quite literally plugged into the wall and charged like a phone. Choose a visualization that resonates with you and use this as your go-to visualization for motivation when it is needed.

Positive Goals with Mantras

Setting goals is a great way to stay motivated to move forward. Choose goals that are built with the SMART acronym: specific, measurable, attainable, realistic, and time-lined. Then, create a mantra to go with each goal. Your mantra should be something empowering, positive, and uplifting. It should be charged with power, allowing you to feel confident and ready to move forward at any given time. Say it with conviction when you do, and watch how much it changes your life.

Chapter 7: Understanding Others

A large part of how we feel is influenced by others and how they have treated us. Often, we are treated in a way that we do not understand, and in many cases, we take it personally as though the person is trying to hurt us intentionally. We may see it as though they do not like us, or as though we are worthless and therefore we deserve to be treated poorly. The reality is actually neither of these. In most cases, it is the complete opposite. You can learn more about this when you learn to understand other people.

Why Should I Understand?

When someone has hurt us, we often feel like they do not deserve anything from us. "They have hurt me; why should I take the time to understand their mean actions?" we might think. These types of thoughts may seem justified, but the reality is that they do not serve you, nor anyone else. Instead, they hold you back from forgiveness, and further, internalize what the other person has done to you. As a result, you will likely feel as though you are personally victimized by the person when in reality their actions have had nothing to do with you at all.

Even when we are incredibly hurt or wronged by someone, their actions are rarely intended to hurt *us*. Instead, they are a reflection of what the other person is feeling inside and what they have been influenced to believe about themselves, others, and the world in general. It can be extremely difficult not to take it personally when someone says or does something harsh toward you, but the reality is that it is never actually intended to hurt you. Instead, the person is reflecting what they believe to be true, and unfortunately, you have been caught in the crossfires of their seemingly direct and pointed actions.

Let's take a look at some common situations where people reflect their own pain onto others. You have likely experienced or witnessed all or most of these yourself:

- Someone has a fight with their spouse at home, then comes to work and takes it out on coworkers or employees.
- Someone is sexually abused at home and goes out to sexually abuse someone else because they believe it to be acceptable or normal.
- Someone witnesses one parent abusing the other parent throughout their childhood and goes on to abuse others or allow others to abuse them because they believe it is acceptable or normal.
- Someone who is having a bad day cuts someone else off when they are driving and gives them the finger, despite that person not having done anything wrong in the situation.
- Someone calls another person ugly and judges their physical appearance because they are not comfortable

with their own appearances and therefore lack self-confidence.

As you can see, every negative thing people do stems from some form of negative or destructive belief that they have cultivated at some point in their past. It may be that they have witnessed it happen or have experienced it and therefore believe it is okay to do to others, or it may be that they have had a bad day and therefore they believe it is acceptable to blame everyone else and cause others to be inconvenienced because they have been inconvenienced. The person is virtually never trying to harm *you,* they are simply acting out what they believe to be acceptable based on the circumstances they are in.

This does not mean that what has happened is acceptable or is not wrong. It is not intended to erase the damage that was caused to you, or to push you to forgive someone because "it was not their fault." The idea, instead, is to understand that people are not trying to hurt you. Instead, they are hurt, and they are trying to make sense of it or do not realize that their own actions are wrong. Rather than seeking help, they are engaging in destructive behavior as an attempt to fix what has happened.

How Can I Understand?

Learning to understand why other people behave the way they do is not always easy, especially when you have been directly hurt by their actions. Still, it is important that you take the time to understand. This understanding will help *you* make sense of what happened, which allows you to process the experience and naturally go through the emotions that come up. Furthermore, it leads you toward the path of forgiveness. The following actions can help you understand people and their behaviors.

Ask "Why?"

One of the best ways to understand people is to ask yourself "why?" Exploring why they may have behaved like that is a great way to understand why someone has treated you the way they have. Often, people get hung up on the wrong "why". They wonder, "Why me?" rather than, "Why did they think that was okay?" Furthermore, if they do get to the question "Why did they think this was okay?" they often get hung up on their own experiences, and fail to look for the other person's perspective.

It is important to understand that it is okay not to know the exact reason why someone did something. You will likely end up in many circumstances where the other person can't or won't tell you about what hurt them or traumatized them and ultimately resulted in them irrationally acting out in the way they did, that resulted in you getting hurt. Still, you can understand that there is always a "why" and it is never you. Look for the opportunity to gain perspective. Try to see beyond where you have experienced it, and what they may have experienced that lead them here.

See Their Inner Innocence

Believe it or not, everyone is innocent on the inside. This does not mean that they are not guilty of hurting you or anything else. Instead, it means that deep down inside, there is an innocence they have that has been hurt. This innocence has been traumatized, hurt, or exploited, and out of fear, pain, anger, and confusion, they are acting out. Some people act out in a self-destructive manner, such as by addiction or self-harm, whereas others act out in an outwardly destructive manner, such as through violence, crimes, bullying, or even vandalism. These acts are the person's way of trying to justify their innocence being seemingly taken away from them. They are still innocent on the inside, but they feel as though they have been taken advantage of or hurt, much in the way that they have done to you. They are not directly trying to hurt you, they are reenacting, acting on, and trying to understand what has happened to them. This is not about you. It is about them. Try and see the innocence in other people.

Chapter 8: Improving Relationships

Learning to improve your relationships with other people is a great way to help yourself feel better, too. Many of us have toxic relationships that result in us feeling energetically depleted, hurt, victimized, traumatized, or otherwise unwell. Often, we get into these situations when the toxic relationship is with someone whom we crave attention from. It may be someone like a parent or a family member, or it may be someone who symbolizes what we want: like a spouse or friend. Because of our desperation to have these people in our lives, we tend to let them get away with more than they should. As a result, we can find ourselves having toxic relationships with them, and in turn many other people, too.

Learning to improve relationships takes time and practice, as you have to learn to see yourself in a new light in the relationship, and you have to teach someone else to do the same. However, once you understand what is required of you, it becomes significantly easier to do what is needed to be done to succeed.

What Can I Do to Improve Relationships?

You can likely think of a few relationships in your life that you would like to improve. These relationships can be with anyone you can think of, there are no limits on who you care about or who you want to have a more positive and healthy relationship with. Once you have considered who, you need to pay attention to the following practices and begin implementing them in your relationship.

Boundaries

Upholding boundaries is extremely important when you are improving relationships with the people in your life. At first, not everyone is going to take to new boundaries well. This is especially true if the person is particularly toxic and has a tendency to disrespect boundaries in general. Still, improving your relationship requires you to set boundaries. You should consider what boundaries need to be set, and then begin upholding them to the best of your ability as soon as you have set these boundaries. There does not need to be any conversation, discussion, or considering anyone else's needs or feelings. Boundaries are about you. They are to protect you, your energy, your wellness, and your rights in your relationship with the other person. Once you have chosen your boundaries, you need to practice enforcing them with others and with yourself. It may take a while, but stay committed to the practice and soon enough you will be effortlessly upholding your boundaries, and other's will be respecting them. Stay committed.

Letting Go of the Past

We often tend to want to move forward with relationships, but we struggle to effectively let go of the past and stop holding people accountable for things they did before. In many cases, years can go by, and we still hold people responsible for something they did "that one time." If something big happened that caused pain and you made a conscious decision to forgive them, it is time to practice that forgiveness. You have to consciously let it go and stop holding them hostage for actions they were responsible for long ago. Learn to intentionally move on and give the relationship a fresh start.

Setting New Expectations

Like setting new boundaries, you can also set new expectations in a relationship. For example, if you feel that you are not respected, that you are not cared about, or that you are otherwise not getting your needs met in a relationship, you can set the expectations that these needs will get met. If they are not, set the expectations of what will happen as a natural consequence. Often, that natural consequence is that the relationship will end or that you will spend less time invested in that person as you fill their place with someone who is more generous with their time and compassion. While you should not rely on other people to make you happy, it is not unreasonable to want to be considered and cared for in relationships. Relationships are a large part of our general wellness, and it is important that you set the intention and uphold the expectation that the relationships in your life will be healthy and positive.

The Golden Rule

Lastly, you should consider the golden rule. Yes, this is the one you have known all along. It is: treat others as you want to be treated. If you want other people to treat you lovingly and with respect, you need to do the same for them. If you want them to uphold boundaries and respect your wishes, you need to do the same for them. You cannot expect people to treat you differently and to respect your new boundaries and expectations if you are not willing to return the same to them. This requires you to take responsibility and become accountable for anything you might be doing that is contributing to your current relationship. It is not comfortable, and it is not easy, but it is mandatory if you will have success with improving the relationships in your life.

Chapter 9: Forgiveness

Forgiveness is a powerful tool that we have access to, that we very rarely take the time to understand and use. Forgiveness is everything you expect it to be and yet nothing like what you thought it would be. It is not easy, it is not always clean and pretty, but it is necessary. When we don't forgive, we are the ones who suffer. And, if we choose to keep a relationship with the person whom we are not forgiving, that relationship will suffer, too.

Learning to forgive requires you to forgive two people: others, and yourself. There are many positive benefits of forgiveness and many negative side effects for choosing not to forgive. It is important that you take the time to learn this lesson and learn to give forgiveness when it is needed.

Why Forgiveness?

Forgiveness is the act of releasing the negative emotions attached to something that has happened in the past. It is not the act of affirming that what someone else did was acceptable or okay. Rather, it is the act of affirming that you understand they are a human and make mistakes and that you are willing to let it go. You can choose whether or not you will maintain a relationship with the person afterward or not. That is completely up to you. However, the act of forgiveness is vital.

When we don't forgive, we are the ones who get hurt. We hurt through anger, hatred, and the feeling that we need to make the other person suffer for what they have done to us. It hurts us more than it hurts them because we live with that anger daily. They, however, only live with it when we expel it onto them. Otherwise, they generally move on and forget about what happened. They may even move on entirely, leaving you in their wake to deal with this leftover emotion that they are no longer present to take from you.

For so many reasons, you need to learn to forgive. It is vital to your wellbeing that you learn to let things go and move on. This will allow you to free up space in your heart and mind to welcome in positive, happy things and let go of negative, painful and hateful things. When you try to get revenge on someone, the only person who feels the wrath of that revenge is you.

How Can I Forgive?

Forgiveness can be hard. When you think of the ways someone has wronged you, it can seem impossible to let it go. People who you care about and who love you may hurt you. People you don't know and who are strangers may hurt you. People who you know but who seem to have no part in your life beyond something basic, like a coworker or boss, may hurt you. Anyone can hurt you in your life. Remember, it is never because of you. It is because of them. Unfortunately, you are left to deal with the aftermath. Here is how you can begin practicing forgiveness.

Forgiving Others: Intentionally Stopping Them from Hurting You

When it comes to forgiving others, it is a good idea to set the intention that you will stop them from hurting you. When you continue to feel pain and hatred, you are essentially giving that person permission to hurt you for much longer than their very actions did. You, in a way, are letting them take up valuable space in your mind and heart, rent-free. You are letting them free-load and hurt you even more, simply because you are not choosing to forgive them and let it go.

Forgiving someone comes in two steps: setting the intention to forgive, and setting the boundaries around the forgiveness. Setting the intention is as simple as deciding to give forgiveness. Setting the boundaries is where you get to determine what action will be taken to uphold the forgiveness. That may be that you do not permit that person to hurt you anymore, so you choose not to keep them in your life or you choose to limit their presence. Or, that may be that you choose that said person may stay in your life but under the notion that they will not hurt you again in that way. You can choose the boundaries, and you are responsible for upholding them. This is your personal choice, so choose as you feel is most comfortable and then commit to your decision.

Forgiving Yourself: Accepting Yourself as You Are

Forgiving yourself is much like forgiving someone else. It is important to understand that you, like others, are only human. You will make mistakes, and things won't always go your way. Still, you need to be willing to try anyway. Learn to accept yourself by accepting that you will make mistakes and things will not always be as you want them to be. Set the intention to forgive yourself for deciding to let go of anything you may have done up until that point to hurt you. Then, set the boundaries that are required to prevent the same hurt from being expelled in the future. Uphold these boundaries with yourself, like you would with anyone else. Some boundaries you may set for yourself include things such as:

- No more negative self-talk or self-hatred.
- No more self-harm or self-sabotaging. If you feel this coming on, you will seek help from now on.
- No more allowing others to do unto you as you have done unto yourself. If you are not allowing yourself to speak negatively toward yourself anymore, do not allow others to, either.
- No more allowing anyone (including yourself) to diminish yourself worth through unkind and thoughtless behaviors.

Setting these boundaries and honoring them is a great way to get serious with yourself and prove to yourself that you are willing to move beyond the acts you have done to hurt yourself and begin healing. Treat your relationship with yourself as you would your relationship with anyone else: be kind, caring, forgiving, nurturing, and empathetic toward yourself.

Chapter 10: The Problem with Marriage Today

It is no secret that there are many issues with modern marriages. We are living in a world where we see family breakdowns as the norm rather than the exception. Illegitimacy and divorce are becoming more widespread than ever before. Despite there being suggestions on ways to update the family model, there are many reasons that modern marriages are nothing less than dysfunctional. Is it any wonder that young adults are confused about marriage?

The life of married couples has drastically changed since the mid-1900's. Marriages used to be seen as a contract that was much more binding than it is today. Society used to have a crystal-clear view of what was acceptable and what generally worked well for successful family dynamics. Divorce was rare and frowned upon, especially by the church. When marriages were facing trouble, couples worked hard to hold those partnerships together. That simple phrase "Till death do us part" was not just a phrase but the first layer of bricks in a marital foundation. It meant everything back in the day.

Over the past few decades, the entire nature of marriage as totally changed. One of the biggest problems that marriages and families face is the face we have become much more approving of staying in long-term relationships without getting married. We somehow view in modern culture that living together is a better alternative to not becoming an added statistic in terms of the divorce rate. Many folks believe that a marriage license does nothing to constitute marriage. This means that without saying "I do" all these couples are taking on the responsibilities that married people have, such a paying bills and dividing household duties.

While many couples are blatantly deciding to skip marriage, there are many others that choose to live together before getting hitched, in an effort to get to know their spouse better. But there is a big problem with this approach. It leads to more divorces since avoiding divorce is a reason to cohabit, to begin with. In fact, the chance of divorce for couples that lived together before getting married is 50%.

So why in the world has the idea of marriage become so unappealing, unsatisfying, and unstable? Many blame it on how easy it is to get a divorce today compared to the past, while others say it is a decline in the desire to get married. Others would argue that there is a major decline in the respect that people have for the institution, even though many couples still express their desire to get married and are still hopeful for the change to create a happy union through the saying of "I do."

There have been many changes to the expectations we have for marriage as well, which set the perfect stage for them to fail and feel unsatisfying. Throughout history, we have expected our spouse to fulfill our needs for pertinent resources, such as food and income, safety and security, and the feeling of being loved. But in "modern marriage," we not only have the expectation for our spouse to facilitate our needs for connections but also to fulfill our needs to further grow and develop. While many couples have become less dependent on their partner for things such as a reliable source of income, we have now become more reliant than ever before on our spouse to meet our desperate need to feel positive self-actualization and self-esteem. In marriages today, our partners are expected to wear many hats, from cheerleaders, challengers, adventurers, confidants, best friends, etc. Plus, add the fact that many couples spend less time with family and friends and you will be able to see why so many start to view marriage as more of a burden than a partnership.

Another issue is that people these days are spending far less time than they should be on providing maintenance to their relationships. It is not a wonder that so many couples are left feeling unsatisfied and wildly disappointed in their marriages.

It is a fact that living within a successful and happy marriage in today's world is challenging. Many people set themselves up automatically to be disappointed, which quickly leads to divorce. Fortunately, there is hope! You have the power to change the way you view and treat your marriage in such modernized times. All it takes is a shift in attitude and actions. When you are able to fully understand the challenges that modern unions face, you are better equipped to combat issues that will inevitably arise.

Chapter 11: Issues That Can Even Threaten Happy Marriages

No matter how hard you try, no one is capable of creating the perfect relationship. Relationships of all labels will not be free of issues all the time. Fruitful marriages take commitment, dedicated work, and reevaluation in the way we communicate, what we expect and what each partner needs to work on. But, we seem to make marriage a heck of a lot harder than it has to be. There are some very common issues that are found among hundreds of thousands of marriages that are more recurring than others.

The future of a marriage is highly dependent on how couples deal with problems that come about, which is why it is not only helpful but valuable to learn about the most common issues that marriages face today. This chapter covers the most prevalent problems that married couples have to face and how you can overcome them before it wrecks a great thing!

Boundary Overstepping

When people get married, more often than not you will find that there is always one of the partners putting extreme effort in changing their spouse. From fundamental beliefs to their sense of fashion, trying to change your partner to better fit your needs is a direct invasion of personal space. When you do this, you are victimizing your partner, which makes them feel hurt and disrespected and sometimes angry.

Overstepping over personal boundaries is usually done intentionally and with a mission in mind. This behavior literally steps all over the idea of having mutual respect for one another, and will eventually result in withdrawal. This behavior makes it difficult for couples to be open with one another and communicate effectively.

On the other hand, it can happen that you unintentionally overstep your spouse's boundaries at time, especially if you are in the process of sincerely attempting to help them. Know when to draw the line when it comes to making changes and pushing for them to avoid total invasion.

Talking versus Communicating

One of the most prominent issues in marriages is believing that talking is communicating, but this is a wrong mindset to have. Things such as complaining and emotional blackmail are not communicating but criticizing. Communicating in a poor manner can lead to major marital issues later down the line.

It is vital to realize that "talking" and "communicating" differ from one another greatly. Talking is providing information without the need for a response, which leaves the opportunity for criticism and complaint. Communicating is both a verbal and nonverbal exchange of information that requires responses. It takes more than one person to properly communicate since it is all about focusing on the connection between the people conversing. Communication is an act where it should be okay to share ideas and information totally free of judgment.

When couples fail to communicate properly, it can be quite easy to make it a habit of ineffectively speaking to one another. If the poorness of communication is not dealt with, it can be a place for future problems to grow. Married folks should really learn how to communicate in order to keep their lives with one another on track and prevent the rising of unnecessary issues.

Decline of Sexual Intimacy

As the honeymoon phase of marriage wears off, life gets back to normal, and there are many reasons as to why couples might lose interest in intimacy from time to time. This is normal. But it is crucial that couples strive to find ways to keep their love life fulfilling and fresh. While sex is a small piece to the marital puzzle, it is unheard of to have a fruitful relationship without it.

Sadly, sex life tends to happen in a vicious cycle if left untouched for too long. It can be challenging to want to have sex when partners feel emotionally detached, but it can hard to feel that needed emotional attachment when there is no physical intimacy. To be able to get past dry spells, couples must be willing to seek out problem areas within the union and work through them to once again become comfortable with one another physically again.

Meandering Focuses

Another issue that many married couples face is a shift in their focus after the marriage is official. When one or both of the partners redirect their attention from the relationship to things such as their jobs, friends, children, hobbies, social activities, etc., it is natural for the other person in the marriage to feel a loss of attention. It is these situations where married folks may start to feel more like roommates than lovers.

It is crucial for both partners to find a balance of interests and the attention they provide their partner. It is encouraged for each people in unions to have their own goals and interests, as long as they are able to fit quality time in with one another.

The main reason this becomes an issue is that one or both parties tend to overreact, which makes both sides feel like they are unable to have a life without their spouse. Understand that your partner has won you, so now is a time to find the balance to grow the marriage as well as pursue other life challenges. Finding a happy medium will help your marriage to grow, as well as be strong enough to support the ambitions of one another.

Emotional Infidelity

It is a very common occurrence that once couples are married that they become emotionally disconnected and unengaged from one another. When this occurs, one or both spouse's needs become unmet, which naturally leads them to look elsewhere to fulfill them. This is where emotional infidelity can make its way into even the happiest of marriages.

Many couples often agree that emotional infidelity is more degrading than cheating physically because it involves much more than just sex, but also the connection with another person on many intimate levels.

To prevent this type of infidelity from happening in your marriage, you both need to be on the same page of what you consider to be "cheating." This will reduce the chance of allowing this to happen in the first place. It is also vital that couples remain tuned in to the emotional needs of one another. If needs are being properly fulfilled, there is no reason that either party should be interested in looking somewhere else.

Financial Disagreements

The bonding of two people also may include the partnering of bank accounts. Even if this is not the case, couples that keep their finances separate still face problems when it comes to finances.

Talking about money can be tense and highly stressful, especially if both partners have different habits with spending and managing their money. When it comes to communicating about finances, it is common for the conversation to be more about habits and personal values than money itself.

Ensure that you and your partner are on the same page when it comes to money and finances. Make it a priority to make a financial plan together so that you can wave any disagreements in the future.

Lack of Appreciation

Conflict feeds on the waning of appreciation in marriages. Both sexes crave recognition, so when couples cease to acknowledge the efforts of their partner, the other will stop those actions that were once appreciated and are now overseen. This can create bitter tension and agitation.

At the beginning of a marriage, both partners make it a priority to show their gratitude for their spouse with loving gestures. But once this stops, those once appreciated actions lose their magic and tend to be seen as a chore more than a choice. No matter how long you and your partner have been together, it is crucial to continue to show your appreciation for the things you both do for one another.

Addiction to Technology

The world today is highly dependent on technology usage, which makes it hard not to get caught up in our electronic devices. This is one of the biggest reasons why couples are reporting unhappiness in marriages these days.

When you begin to interact with friends by phone at the dinner table, you are ignoring your spouse. When you play on your tablet or computer after dinner instead of engaging with your spouse, you are replacing the opportunities for intimacy and healthy communication. If you allow it, technology does have a way of getting between marriages and literally taking it over. It is time to snap back to reality.

Selfishness

If one party in a union continuously puts their needs and desires ahead of their partner's, it is only a matter of time till the other spouse begins to feel unloved and unworthy of their spouse's love. Marriage is built on the foundation of promising to love one another for better or worse. A portion of this promise is to not act in selfish ways. Sounds easy, right?

Despite our best efforts, there are times that selfishness comes in various forms that we fail to recognize right away. Selfishness is a monster that is abusive, possessive, jealous, manipulative and heavily controlling. To opposing parties, it can be seen as disrespect and a lack of consideration.

To prevent selfishness from coming between you and your spouse, each side must learn how to engage with empathy and build a balance to ensure both partners are getting what they need from the marriage.

Lack of Trust

It is safe to say that without trust there is truly no love. It is what makes up a big portion of the foundation of all love, especially in a marriage. Healthy marriages do not exist without trust. When a partner breaks a promise, lies, or cheats, it can drastically hurt or even kill the relationship.

It is not easy to restore trust, and takes commitment from both partners to fix the relationship in order to fulfill prosperity in the union again. If issues are not dealt with they are left to fester, which can cause the betrayed spouse to feel suspicious of the other's actions, angry, and hurt.

The Changes of Future Ambitions

When couples go to get married, they are often on the same page and path with what they want for their futures. The reason this is such a common issue is that life brings about changes and one or both partners change their minds and start to fulfill new ambitions. This is why it is vital to keep lines of communication open so that if one or both of you do change your mind, you can avoid the change in ambitions from being a shocking awakening to your partner.

Inability to Forgive

One of the biggest roots of problematic issues in marriages is the lack of willingness or the total inability to forgive each other. From petty to traumatic offenses, 90% of the issues within partnerships are due to the inability to forgive themselves, their spouse, or other people that have impacted their lives in negative ways.

No worries, there is an entire chapter dedicated to forgiveness. Even the most intense of problems can be properly forgiven over time.

Within the remaining chapters of this book, you will find valuable insight, information, tips, methods, and techniques on how you can revive that once beautiful spark between you and your spouse!

Chapter 12: Signs Your Marriage is in Trouble

One of the most painful things in life is seeing the disintegration of a once loving marriage. It is one of the worst emotionally, mentally, and physically painful things you may ever experience in your lifetime.

Instead of accepting defeat and wrecking an aspect of your life that you wanted to be around "Till death do you part," we will start the mending of your marriage by discussing some warning signs that you might be aware of or you have yet to take notice of.

Arguing about same subjects

All marriages inevitably face challenges and disputes from time to time, but if you find that you and your partner are constantly bantering about the same subjects on a regular occasion, this could be a major red flag. If you continuously are unable to find a compromise to agree to disagree, then you will both constantly struggle to maintain a strong relationship.

Constantly saying ugly things to one another

Always thinking with an argumentative tone to one another is mean and leads to hurt feelings. In fact, contempt is the number one predictor of a path being paved towards divorce. Negative and sly commentary, hostile remarks, teasing, sarcasm, teasing, mocking and disrespectful words, as well as negative body language all, lead to the poisoning of marriages.

No responsibility taken

One of the main things that put your marriage automatically on the rocks is when neither side takes responsibility for their actions or fails to acknowledge their faults. When people take responsibility during disagreements, this shows a willingness to do what needs to be done in order to save the marriage.

Different intimacy views

If the lines of communication seem to be closed off, then this could mean double trouble for the marriage. When communication is cut off, this eventually leads to a sexless and unpassionate marriage. You must let your spouse know what your needs are and vice versa.

Constant suspicion of one another

A partnership without trust will never last. It is what makes the foundation for all kinds of relationships in our lives stable and healthy. You marriage will inevitably struggle if you are always wondering if your partner has your best interest in mind and will never do anything to deceive or hurt you.

No longer go on dates

Ask yourself how long you have had one-on-one time with your spouse, time without any distractions? Five minutes, an hour, perhaps less? If you and your spouse no longer spend quality time together without distractions, you should make it a top priority to make each other a priority in your lives.

Happier and content being apart than with each other

Marriages that are healthy involve two people that genuinely like spending quality time with one another. If you or your spouse find that you are happier away from each other than when you are together, then there are some underlying problems that have the potential to shake things up in your marriage negatively. Time spent together is needed to develop both physical and emotional connections that are crucial to a healthy and happy partnership.

Dishonesty about finances

Like you have read several times before already, relationships without trust and transparency is like trying to drive to a destination without any gas. You will only sit in the car, but fail to go anywhere. Even if you push and shove that car, you will not get far whatsoever. If you or your spouse lies, hides, or gambles away your money, don't hesitate to confront them about the issue. You need to have peace of mind that your spouse has your back and is willing, to be honest with you no matter what.

Cannot agree on compromises

If neither party in a marriage is unable to find compromise in order to solve issues, this will eventually result in hefty escalations. You will find that over time your fights grow more intense and tend to hurt worse. If you find yourself trying to keep your head above water when it comes to finding a balance, continue speaking in a respectful manner to one another till you both can find a solution you can both feel content with.

Don't allow one another time to spend with others

Your marriage is in trouble if you find that your spouse fails to let you spend time with family, friends, co-workers and other people. Healthy marriages have no place for possessive behavior.

Thoughts about being unfaithful

Even having an inkling of being unfaithful can be a cause for major trouble. It is not okay for either party to let eyes wander to other people. You should only seek excitement within your marriage and never from other external sources.

Flirting online

If either party in a marriage flirts with others online, then it is likely that the marriage is unstable. Even if you have never met or plan to meet the people you are talking to via the internet, your thoughts that are devoted to people other than your spouse can be greatly considered as an emotional affair.

Only communication being superficial topics

If you find that the only conversations you have with your spouse are trivial in nature, it can be a very bad sign. Healthy marriages have conversations that do much more than scratch the surface of the real thoughts and feelings both parties have. Open communication is a fantastic way to feel connected with your spouse on an intellectual and emotional level. Make it a priority to discuss feelings, concerns, ambitions, and goals. This is a key to a long-lasting marriage.

Feeling of worthlessness

If you find that criticism is always coming between you and your spouse, this could mean trouble. It's vital for each spouse to have the confidence that they have your back and are there to support you. Don't allow yourself to be a partner's doormat. You should never feel patronized or belittled. If you constantly feel like you are not enough for your spouse, take the time to talk to them to get to the core of the issue.

Shame on one another

Having disgust and shame towards each other should not be allowed in any marriage. Accusations against the character and intentions of your spouse are harmful to your willingness to sustain a lasting partnership.

Feeling of loneliness even when spouse is present

If you feel lonely even when your partner is sitting right next to you, this means that there is more than likely a lack of connection between you and your spouse. Make it a priority to cultivate a marriage of not only a friendship but of deep connection.

Make decisions based on yourself

At the beginning of a marriage, you find that you ask your partner for their opinion, point of view, and expertise on various subjects. It is when you find yourself making decisions without considering the feelings of your spouse or how it may affect them that trouble starts.

Being tallying

If you are finding that you and your spouse are constantly keeping tally and keeping a conscious mental note on how much you contribute to the marriage, this can be a cause for major agitation.

Teammates to roommates

Teammates work together to accomplish goals, sharing ideas on how they can succeed and envision their lives, home, and plans together. Roommates, however, act on singular projects with no thought or act of respect towards one another. They take care of their own space, acting out on separate plans, which eventually become their separate lives.

Removal of knives in the back to hurt one another

Those who have been in relationships with another human being long enough are consciously aware of the buttons they do not like being pushed. You have found ways to avoid pushing those buttons. But, as a marriage wears on, you find that you intentionally press them and actually like pestering them.

Call yourself king or queen of the home

In a fruitful marriage, no needs are more important than others. The desires of two people are split equally and you both attempt to fulfill one another's needs. But as life goes on, stress and resentment can cause tension, making you feel like your needs and desires take priority.

Immediate family chooses sides instead of fighting for common ground

You will find that with miscommunication and disrespect are right alongside with your immediate family members choosing to pick "upsides" during conversations and debates. The matter of winning or losing becomes the mission instead of shooting for compromise. This leads to both you and your spouse isolating one another from friends and family.

One of the worst things that can happen is letting your marriage become just as dysfunctional as the display of division between the lack of misunderstanding among family members. The unity of family disintegrates, which leads to major family feuds, which is terrible for any sort of healthy marriage.

Chapter 13: Rebuilding Your Marriage After an Affair

There are few to no marital issues that cause as much devastation and heartache as infidelity, an action that totally undermines the foundation of the sanctity of marriage. Cheating can bring about damaging consequences to a married couple and is more often than not a deal breaker that results in a divorce. But there are many couples that decide to weather out the aftermath of hurricane infidelity rather than part ways.

Understanding Infidelity

Adultery cannot be defined by a clear or single situation. In fact, what is considered as cheating varies greatly among couples. Is an emotional connection with no physical ties with someone outside the marriage considered cheating? What about relationships with people online? Every person and couple need to clearly communicate what they individually and together consider to be infidelity within their marriage.

Reasons Affairs Occur

There is a plethora of factors that can contribute to the happening of infidelity and surprisingly, many have nothing to do with sexual intimacy.

- Marital issues that have been left unaddressed for years
- Addiction to alcohol, drugs, gambling, sex, etc.
- Mental health problems like bipolar disorder, learning disabilities, ADD, anxiety, depression, etc.
- Physical health problems, such as disability or chronic pain
- Communication breakdowns that are caused by emotional and needs of the relationship
- Reduction of fondness
- Loss of caring for one another
- Lack of overall affection

The Discovery of an Affair

When one initially discovers that an affair has been happening behind their back, it can trigger very powerful emotions for both partners in the marriage. Emotions such as remorse, guilt, depression, shame, anger, and betrayal can create an ugly head between a couple. It can be challenging to think clearly in order to make decisions that decide the long-term of a marriage. Here are a few things to consider:

- <u>Don't be rash</u>: If you think that the buildup of emotions might lead to you physically hurting yourself, your partner, or anyone else, seek professional assistance right away.

- <u>Provide space</u>: Finding out about affairs is intense. You will find yourself thinking erratic thoughts and feel very unlike yourself as you try to grasp the severity of what has occurred. Avoid intense discussions so you can begin the mending process.

- <u>Find support</u>: Find trusted loved ones and/or friends that you can share your feelings and experience with. Find people who will support, encourage, and help you through the healing process. Avoid those who you think will be biased, critical, or too judgmental. Spiritual leaders might be a good place to start since they are trained and have experience with marriage issues.

- <u>Don't rush:</u> You may have a very deep need to understand what has happened in your marriage, but you must do your best to not dive into intimate details of the affair. Do so only with professional guidance. Otherwise, you might totally burn what is left of the bridge between you and your partner.

Steps to Mending a Marriage After an Affair

The process of mending after cheating or emotional infidelity doesn't happen quickly. Even those that are dedicated to making things work after the fact end up with waylaid feelings, resentment, and guilt that paralyzes.

For the person who cheated, it is natural to think things like "How did I get here?" or "I didn't see this coming..." No matter what exactly led you down the path to being unfaithful, there will come a point where it is time to wake-up, face the music and acknowledge what happened, especially how devastating your choices can be.

If you and your partner desire to pursue the healing process after infidelity, here are vital steps to take in order to emerge as an even stronger couple in your marriage after an affair.

- **End the Affair**

The one who cheated needs to cease all contact with the person they were unfaithful with. No quick meet-ups, phone calls, texts, and especially no romantic or sexual contact. If the other person does make contact, tell your spouse about it before they ask. This is the first step to rebuilding trust in the marriage.

- **Be Honest**

For many people on the other side of cheating, they need the wronged spouse to spew into detail about the affair. It is also crucial that the hurt partner feels heard, especially since it is easy to feel like they are crazy when grieving. When they ask you about the affair, be brutally honest. This might bring about more pain at first, but it will help later down the line as you mend your relationship. This might seem very counterintuitive, but it is vital in order to rebuild trust. Tell them the entire truth about the affair and be as transparent as possible. Explain to them how it came about and how you ended it. This gives the hurt spouse a timeline to feel confident that you are no longer hiding secrets from them. Be totally open to them asking you questions that pertain to your whereabouts. Transparency is crucial to the mending process.

Protect Your Spouse from Sexual Details

Although total transparency is critical to being honest, giving away too many details in regard to the sexual intimacy of the affair will give your spouse images that they do not need to think about. If you must, seek the help of a counselor to walk you through this process. They will be able to decipher information that is useful and what is hurtful.

Take Responsibility

Along with honesty comes taking total responsibility for the affair. Even though there were probably underlying issues in the marriage that initiated the seeking of infidelity, the cheating spouse was the one who acted upon it. They betrayed the vows of marriage, despite the issues in it. It is very easy to slide right into the game of blame, but a vital step is knowing the choice you made and putting excuses and scapegoats to the side.

Empathize and Bear Witness to the Hurt Partner

It is natural for the hurt party to have emotional responses to your act of unfaithfulness. In order to mend together, you must be willing to seek how it must feel to be the betrayed spouse. This is no time to demand that they own their faults that might have caused you to make poor decisions. At this point, you must establish the commitment you have to the marriage.

Being empathetic can lead to heartfelt forgiveness. In fact, one of the best indicators that your marriage will survive this fallout is if the unfaithful partner shows empathy towards the one they betrayed.

Yes, it is also natural for the unfaithful spouse to want to fight back to defend their reasoning, but there is no place for that at this point. They must sit back and try to understand how their spouse feels. Validate their pain by showing tenderness and compassion. Understand the choices you made have caused a great deal of turmoil in your marriage. It is challenging, but allow them as much space and time as they need to process the deep tides of emotions they are feeling and respond to their woes with regret and honesty.

Make the Commitment to Recommit to Your Spouse

Clarify to your spouse that you are dedicated to fight for your marriage. You have deeply burned the bridge of trust between the two of you and realize that rebuilding it will take time. The steps you take now must be proactive, which is crucial to the recovery of your relationship.

Write an Apology

Once the cheating spouse has listened and understood their partner's declaration of their emotionally-fueled feelings, it is recommended by many professionals that the cheater writes out the account in their own words. Writing a less that gives details and specific points proves that they do grasp the sorrow they have caused thanks to their actions. Don't use "I'm sorry" a lot, it won't get you far. Use verbal reassurances and make promises that something this detrimental won't occur again. A written apology must prove that they have taken the time to understand what the hurt spouse is feeling. This means citing examples of how they have hurt their spouse and taking actions to prove that it will not happen again in the future.

Avoid "Cheap Forgiveness"

The desire to salvage the marriage after infidelity can be overwhelming, which can cause the need to vent anger to be pushed to the side. The wronged partner then forgives their unfaithful spouse before they have a chance to seethe. This behavior does more harm than good and is seen often in people who are simply scared of being alone rather than the consequences of forgiving a cheating partner too soon. "Cheap forgiveness" not only swindles the wronged partner from undergoing the grieving process, but it sets up the relationship to experience future infidelities when they do not force their spouse to grasp the pain they have caused.

Share the Responsibility

Infidelity (usually) occurs with only one partner in the marriage. Even though it is the fault of one person for acting unfaithfully, there are oftentimes reasons that both parties of a marriage hold blame for cheating occurring. The one who was unfaithful should own up to 100% of their guilt since no one forced them to cheat, but the wronged spouse should also acknowledge how they played a role in fostering this to happen. It is important that both partners must see how they had a hand in creating the isolation and loneliness that compelled their spouse to seek intimacy elsewhere.

Set Boundaries and Rules

To allow the marriage to recover from the blow of infidelity, there must be ways to grant and earn trust back. Establish rules that are non-negotiable at the very start of the healing process. It can include things such as:

- The wronged spouse requesting that their spouse always answer their phone, even if they are in a place that a full conversation cannot be had

- If infidelity happened online, the hurt spouse could make a rule to look over their partner's shoulder when they are on the computer.

Though these sounds a little unorthodox, bringing an imbalance of power eases the insecure feelings and the mistrust that the hurt party has. It also proves that the cheating partner is willing to give up their right to privacy while their partner regains the confidence in their marriage.

Healing of the Cheater's Heart

Even though the spouse who was unfaithful was in the wrong, they will also experience a world of emotion. From unworthiness, guilt, and shame, these negative emotions can keep the marriage from the healthy mending it needs to survive. Marriages that last are made up of two healthy individuals. So the cheater may need outside help in order to become healthier mentally to partake in the sustainability of a long-lasting marriage after infidelity.

Express Gratitude

If you have made it this far in married life after infidelity, then you know that the wronged spouse is fighting to keep the marriage despite the cheater's past choices. This is an act of a sacrificial love, which means you should be showing major actions of how grateful you are that they love you enough to keep you around.

Redefine Sexual Intimacy

After dealing with the hurricane of emotions, the next biggest hurdle in healing a marriage after an affair lies between the sheets. It often feels as though the person your partner cheated with is lying right in-between you, a ghost that strains sexual relations.

This can mean major trouble in this aspect of the marriage. The spouse that was unfaithful may feel pressured to please their partner, which leads to low-performance thanks to distraction. Then the hurt partner, who is already heavily insecure, interprets the low performance as a lack of attraction and interest.

Remember that it takes time to regain the passion that your marriage once had, especially after infidelity. It's important to express desires and fears, which eventually will lead to vulnerability in a physical manner, which can foster sexual intimacy.

Ignore Common Perceptions of Cheaters

We frequently hear the phrase, "once a cheater, always a cheater." This assumption is dangerous in terms of rebuilding a marriage. Plus, many people who have cheated think that because of perceptions like this, that they may be susceptible of cheating on their spouse again in the future. Inevitably, there will be folks that cheat again. But remember that there are people that act upon it once and never think about doing it again. They have learned their lesson.

This being said, while you should ignore common aphorisms, it is vital to remember that if the adulterer is not willing to listen to the hurt spouse speak of their experience with the pain of infidelity, it may be a red flag that it is not worth the time and effort it takes to rebuild trust.

Reality Check

The aftermath of hurricane infidelity can lead to the feeling that a marriage is dysfunctional. A unique point of view is to remember that many long-term couples experience at least one instance of infidelity in some form or another and manage to make it through. The stigma of adultery keeps this rising issue on the DL, but despite the negativity that surrounds the marriage after the fact, there are numerous couples that come out of an affair closer and more honest than they were before!

Marriages can greatly benefit from trust-building and emotional closures, no matter if it is infidelity or something else that sparks this crucial development.

Letting Go

It's important to remember that healing a marriage after infidelity not only takes the opening up of the cheater but of the spouse that was hurt by this experience as well. The wronged partner must be willing to loosen the leash of pain over time and allow the trust to grow. The restoration of a marriage relies on both parties to prove that they are willing to put new energy into the relationship. This requires both partners to take risks. It is also pertinent to remember that this process takes time. There will be days that it feels like the two of your make leaps and bounds, while other days you feel that you both are pushed back to square one.

Affairs give marriages major shock waves for months to years. But it is more than possible to restore and totally rebuild the marriage to be greater than it was before infidelity occurred. The road to recovery is anything but easy, but if you are both it in for the long haul, it can be an unexpected gift that your marriage needed all along. If you both push through it, a stronger, better union can emerge.

Mistakes in Rebuilding Marriages

Infidelity is a total violation of boundaries in a relationship. Therefore, many people think that imposing tighter restrictions and boundaries to prevent it from happening again seem like the way to go. But this is by no means effective in the long run. Why? Because affairs don't just occur in bad marriages. They can happen in good ones too. This means infidelity is not the problem, but rather just a symptom of the real issue.

When marriages are faced with cheating, two common questions are asked:

1. *What went wrong to make this happen?*
2. *Why did I not see this coming?*

These are natural, but then to fix what is wrong and to prevent it from happening again, many couples make one of these mistakes:

1. They overcorrect by being too controlling
2. They overcompensate by changing too much

Obviously, both of these approaches can majorly backfire. Why? Because affairs can be usually attributed to four key things, also known as the 'ABC's of Infidelity.'

Before we talk about these ABC's, I want to introduce you to something referred to as "The Broken Windows Theory." It represents that having a broken window in your home would make it much more likely for someone to break in with ease, even though a window is not a cause for a break in. This is the same logic that applies to the ABC's of Infidelity.

There are four specific things that make a marriage vulnerable to cheating:

- **A** represents "*attention*," or therefore heavily lacking. It can make people very vulnerable to temptations.

- **B** represents "*boredom*," or couples in a marriage taking things for granted. A lack of newness in a relationship is a main reason why affairs occur, rather than a lack of love. Even the best of relationships are not immune to boredom.

- **C** represents too much "*control*." Either partner being too controlling can be perceived by both as a major lack of freedom in a marriage, which makes people more likely to rebel against one another. This is why so many affairs are based on revenge.

- **C** represents not enough "*communication*," which can easily create rifts in a marriage of any kind.

Mistake #1: Over-correction by too much control

Let's take it a step further and consider how infidelity could be a way that a spouse controls the other. We all have hard-wired needs, one of the biggest being the need for self-expression and freedom. Freedom to some is seen as just an American value when really it is a human *need*. We all desire the freedom to express our individuality, the freedom to say no, to choose, and to change our minds.

The issue is, however, that it can be rather challenging to balance the need for free with our need for safety. In an effort to make these needs meet, couples suffocate one another. This is the beginning of the stifling of each other's independence.

We can sit there and imagine and think that is it possible to control another person, but in reality, it's not. You are able to control people as much as you are capable of controlling the weather, which is not at all. In an effort to create safety, all that controlling often just lead to rebellion and stagnation. This means it's only a matter of time before each spouse resents one another.

Even if you have the best of intentions, trying your hardest to create a safety net within your marriage often leads to an excessive amount of control that leads to the breaking of those windows we spoke about earlier. This means that many affairs are simply an act of rebellion, a spouse's moment of defiance, or a passive-aggressive way to push against the feeling of being too controlled. Control of any kind doesn't make security, but rather compliance. Defiance lurks right underneath compliance. So, remember this rule if you want to avoid falling into this controlling trap:

Rule #1: *Fidelity is a choice <u>and</u> a commitment that cannot be forced or enforced*.

The bad news is your spouse will be faithful by choice. This means you cannot demand their loyalty to you. All you can do is *inspire* it. The good news? There *is* a lot you can do to inspire this type of fidelity and devotion in your marriage. Shift focus from attempting to control and learn ways to rekindle the desire within one another. This is the way to instill loyalty, monogamy, and faithfulness for life.

Mistake #2: Overcompensation by too much change

This mistake is a classic one that is created by a lack of knowledge of what exactly went wrong to lead to an affair. Couples tend to make the assumption that everything was wrong, therefore, making way too many changes all at once in an effort to create something new from the crumbled marriage after Hurricane Affair.

I am sure you have heard of 'open marriages,' where couples agree to go against the tradition of monogamy and give one another permission to engage in extramarital affairs. Is this better in terms of preventing infidelity than traditional rules of a monogamous marriage? You may be surprised to find out that both open and traditional marriages are susceptible to adultery. Why? Because any sort of partnership relies heavily on transparency and honesty. Deception is the enemy in both of these types of marriages.

So, *is* there a way to have the benefits of monogamy while taking advantage of the adventure and novelty that open marriages offer? Yes, there is! Which leads us to the other rule:

Rule #2: Strong marriages are not created by default, but rather by design.

Customizing your marriage will help you and your spouse to keep the traditional boundaries you desire intact, while still leaving room for spontaneity, newness, and expansion. It is not all about making changes but making the right changes. While you should never ignore the things that might make your vulnerable, you should also not overreact either. Corrections and adjustments need to be made, but be mindful of them so that you are not overcompensating or correcting the situation by acting upon the wrong things and making the affair situation worse.

Sit down with your partner and discuss the kinds of changes you both would like to see. This will help to decipher the things you both value in a relationship. This means taking the time to ask those tough questions and making a dedicated effort to customize the rules to fit into *your* marriage.

Chapter 14: Unexpected Ways to Improve Your Marriage

It's no secret that it takes two loving people to become a couple, fall in love, and say "I do." But when it comes to bettering the relationship, it only takes one person. If you are constantly waiting for your spouse to take the reins to better your marriage, then you are responsible for helping cook a recipe for unhappiness that may lead to divorce.

There are many things you can do every day to improve your marriage, which can be looking at yourself and changing your own behavior. This chapter brings to light unique methods of saving your marriage.

If you are in a marriage where the both of you have the basics covered, there are other things you can do to make it last effectively through the wear and tear of the years to come. All of these methods are ways to provide a spark and improve the overall quality of your marriage.

Ignore experts

While this might seem quite counterintuitive, you would be surprised just how effective thinking about what makes your spouse happy can really do to improve your relationship. Instead of seeking out an expert for advice and spending hundreds of dollars of your hard-earned money, start doing the things that make your spouse smile or will delight them. From cleaning trash out of the car to taking the chore of waking the kids up, start doing them now!

Invent an imaginary houseguest

When you have family, friends, or other guests at your home, you tend to think and act differently with your partner than usual, especially when you disagree. Take advantage of this fact next time you want to scream at one another. Imagine someone is staying in the room next to yours. This will help you to both think deeper about what you want to say and surprisingly relieve some tension that arguments create. This will encourage you to be more kind to your spouse, even when they have done something to upset you.

Stop correcting unrelated errors

There is no reason to dwell on things your spouse does wrong to the point of bringing up factors that make no difference. For example, it simply does not matter if there were 50 or 75 guests at a wedding when you are discussing that they have too much to drink.

Praise and love specifically

Saying things like, "You are so awesome, and I love you" is not necessarily a bad thing, but it could be more sufficient. Think back to the early days of your relationship with your partner. This is where you will find the qualities that attracted you to them in the first place. But the longer people are together, the less likely they are to mention these details that once meant the world to them.

Think about how specific your daily criticisms are, such as "Why did you put so much water in this pot?" or "You came home with six bananas when I just needed three!". Use that the tendency to be specific for when you praise your partner as well.

Put limits on listening

Listening is one of the best gifts you can give one another in any kind of relationship. It is something that many of us do not do enough of. However, there are times that a limit should be put to listening. There are times that you are doing so many things at once, from watching the kids to cooking to watching the news all at once, that sincerely listening to your partner as they try to speak to you about something simply doesn't work. Articulate a quick and calm sentence to inform them that you will be happy to listen to them later, such as "I am super busy right now, but will be happy to talk later."

Don't use the word 'foreplay'

All couples, married or not, need to make it a priority to talk about sex. But that is no reason to bring back "The Joy of Sex" '70's vocabulary. Terms like 'foreplay' are not sexy. It also suggests that anything you do besides sex is not a real thing, and any other actions are just something you do to get ready for the act of sex.

Invite what you dread

If you are tired of hearing your spouse continuously talk about how worried they are about their mom in the nursing home, perhaps it is time that you start up the conversation. It is natural to worry that you might open up emotional wounds with your partner, but there are times that you must be willing to talk about subjects you dread. You will find though that your spouse worries less about these sorts of issues if they see that you are ready to invite them to tell you everything all in one moment. You do not have to be their cheerleader, but just be a good listener.

Use 'I-statement' wisely

The technique of using I-statements requires one to talk about how they feel instead of just what your partner feels. For example, if your spouse is late on a regular basis, instead of saying "It's rude that you are always late," say something like, "It's hard for me to plan dinner when you are late." This opens up a healthier discussion since it does not sound like you are attacking them. Just an FYI, not all I-statements mean that you are referring to yourself. Just remember to avoid commentary like, "I think you are controlling" unless you are looking to start a fight.

Disorient with praise

Instead of fulfilling your spouse's expectations that you will criticize them, surprise them with praise instead. For example, if they have a tendency, if they are often overbearing with their younger sibling and this is something you have previously fought over, say something such as, "I admire your humor with your brother. It lightens things up, and you are so funny with him." This is unexpected as well as disarming, which encourages new behavior from both parties in a marriage.

Describe with less

When a spouse says that they do not wish to talk or are not good at talking, the real issue usually is they get totally overwhelmed with too much information all at once. For example, instead of going off about multiple things at once, cut off at your point. "You told me you would clean up the kitchen and you haven't." Don't bother tacking on all those other issues you have with them at the moment.

Have secrets

Good and open communication is vital to a healthy marriage, but so is keeping certain things to yourself as well. For instance, if you start to get a small crush on a new coworker at the office, don't mention it to your partner. Or if you have your own bank account, they do not need to know how much you spent on that new gadget. You will both be more content if you do not mention these tiny, innocent discrepancies.

Tell lies

Honesty is the best policy, but there are some circumstances that lying will benefit the relationship. Don't blatantly tell your partner "yes" if they ask if they look fat when trying on an outfit. There are times that giving your spouse an ego boost is much more important than the truth.

Don't share

It is crucial to talk to your spouse about your interests, ideas, dreams, plans and about the day you had. But it is not necessary to tell them every single detail or thought you had. No one likes to listen to someone go on and on about the minute detail of a boring workday. If you are someone that finds themselves complaining a lot, this kind of sharing only bring your spouse down. Unless you are having an extremely bad day, do not overload your partner with your frustrations.

Have separate lives

This does not mean going out and starting a secret family. Spending time together is important, but there is such a thing as being together too much. The more time you spend with each other, the less you experience alone, and the less you have to tell your spouse. Neediness and dependence on a partner are wildly unattractive, but the opposite is true about people with a degree of independence. Have your own hobbies, interests, and friends. This will help to keep a spark of interest and the attraction you have for one another alive.

Be selfish

Keeping the spark of love alive takes compromise, tolerance, and patience. None of that is a bad thing! But this does not mean that you should give up on your own needs. While it may feel good to compromise all the time or for your spouse to have their own way, they will lose respect for you over time if you continue to be a doormat, especially if you are unhappy deep down. For the sake of your marriage, learn to be selfish on occasion.

Be irresponsible

Responsibilities, like paying the bills and taking care of the kids, is important, but it's equally as crucial to take time to shake off worries and cares and act like a teenager again. Do something a bit crazy with your partner encourages the creation of new memories that will keep you going when life gets serious. This is especially important to do while you are still young and capable of getting into a bit of mischief.

Forego Valentine's Day

Learn early on how your spouse feels about holidays like Valentine's Day. It is a safe bet to still have a backup plan if they expect something, but if you are like me, I strongly dislike the commercialism and consumerism of the holiday. Discuss it and make a pact if you can to ignore the holiday. Laugh and wish one another a happy Valentine's Day, but make the love you have for one another really count the other 364 days of the year. Romantic gestures are a great thing, but you should show your spouse that you love them each and every day. You

can't just buy a pricey gift one day out of the year to make up
for the other days of ignoring them.

Chapter 15: Bringing Love Back into Your Marriage

After you have been married to your partner for a while, you find that the majority of your conversations are centered around the kids, chores, work and other mundane aspects of everyday life. With the hustle, bustle and endless stress of day to day responsibilities, it can be challenging to keep the same loving feelings you both felt when you said, "I do" intact.

One of the biggest reasons that couples lose their passion is because of a 'pursuer-distancer' patterns that seem to naturally take place over time. This is a demand-withdraw pattern where one spouse becomes too aggressive and/or critical, and the other typically becomes distance and defensive. There are many couples that get stuck in this detrimental pattern. It has been shown that 80% of these couples get divorced within their first 4-5 years of living the married life.

It is nearly impossible and otherwise irresponsible to go on impromptu vacations or skip performing responsibilities to spend hours in bed. But there are some other exciting and fun techniques that are successful in bringing back the spark into your marriage. Make it a priority to challenge yourself to fall back in love with your spouse with the unique and fun methods outlined in this chapter!

Ways to Rekindle Sexual Passion

Promote emotional intimacy

All sexually healthy relationships are founded upon closeness. If you want to improve the physical aspects of your marriage, you must be willing to work on strengthening your emotional connection with your spouse. Focus on not only meeting the needs of your partner but effectively communicating your own needs in a respectful way.

If you are looking to add a spark to the passion that you once had, you must remember to turn towards one another. Practice emotional attunement in order to stay connected, even in times of disagreement. This means you must tune in to one another by a show of empathy rather than becoming defensive. Both spouses should speak about the way they feel in a positive way.

The expressing of positive needs is a part of the recipe needed for a successful and long-lasting partnership for both the speaker and the listener. This is because it conveys requests as well as complaints without blame and criticism. This means both parties will have to be willing to do the work in order to mentally transform their thoughts of what is wrong with one another to what they can provide to one another.

Revive intimate chemistry

During the first phases of marriage, couples are excited about falling in love. However, this state of bliss eventually fades. Science and the natural functioning of our bodies have a lot to do with this. At the beginning of relationships, the bonding hormone, oxytocin is released, causing infatuation that makes both parties feel turned on by touch and somewhat euphoric. Like a drug, it gives partners an immediate reward which also helps us to feel bonded to them.

Hugs, hand holding, and other tender touches are fantastic ways to reaffirm your love for your spouse. Physical affection is part of setting the stage for sexual pleasure. Set a goal to double the time you spend performing sensual touches, hugging and kissing, especially if you are looking to improve your marriage.

Sexual attraction is certainly not easily maintained over time. Many lose this passion because both sides are not willing to give up the control they have and show their vulnerable side. Many other sexual concerns are born from interpersonal issues within the marriage itself.

Change the way sex is initiated

Avoid playing the blame game and learn to mix things up in order to end the power struggle. Those who are distancers should practice initiating sex and those that play the role of pursuer should find ways to tell their spouse how sexy they are without the demand of being close.

Hold hands more

Even the simplest of touches like hugging and holding hands releases oxytocin, which then causing a sensation of calmness. It is also released during sexual orgasm as well. Physical affection helps to reduce hormones caused by stress. So why not hold those beautiful hands more?

Let tension build

Believe it or not, we experience much more pleasure when the anticipation of receiving an award is played out for a longer time. Take your sweet time during foreplay; change up locations where you have sex, make it more romantic, and even share each other's sexual fantasies.

Separate time for intimacy from the usual routine

Plan to be intimate and make it a point to not discuss issues within your marriage and everyday things like chores and the kids while in the bedroom. Arousal plummets when we are stressed out and distracted.

Make time to spend with your spouse

Dates are not just for teenagers! Carve out time to court and flirt with your spouse. This helps to initiate sexual intimacy. Also, try out new activities that bring both of you pleasure. In fact, everything you strive to do positively in your marriage each day impacts foreplay.

Hone in on affectionate touches

Give your spouse a back/shoulder rub, hold hands while watching a movie, gently caress their body with your fingertips, etc. Foreplay is associated with sexual intercourse, but affectionate touches are a very powerful way to show your spouse the passion you have for them. It helps to rekindle passion, even in partners that are not huge touchy-feely people.

Practice emotional vulnerability

Learn the importance of openly sharing your desires, fantasies and innermost wishes with your partner, both in bed and in everyday life.

Maintain curiosity

Don't be afraid to try out new ways to bring pleasure to your partner and vice versa. View sex as a time to get to know your spouse better time after time.

Mix up sex

Don't have just one kind of sex all the time, this will become rather boring after a while. Instead, aim to have highly erotic sex one night, more intimate another time, and gentle and tender sex on another occasion. This breaks up the routine and allows you to try new things as your sexual needs and desires change.

Easy Ways to Upgrade Your Marriage

Making your marriage more intimate, connected and secure shouldn't have to be overwhelming. Here are some great tips that lead to reaping the rewards much sooner than you think, while also building a stronger foundation in the long run.

Go to bed together

Sleeping together is both sexy and exciting when you first start dating your partner. But over time and after years of being married, you find that you go to bed at different times or may even sleep in separate beds. Any of these types of things can become a negative routine that you fall into. Going to bed together is something sacred that you only share with your partner. It shouldn't just be about sex, but rather a time that you can have a few intimate moments with them before catching some shuteye. It helps to align your schedules and feel more connected through the act of catching up. Make your bedroom free of cellular devices too, so both of you can be consciously present with one another before shutting out the lights.

Show your love

Love is not just a feeling, but rather a showing of feeling. As time goes on, it takes more effort to show how much you love your spouse. Even the littlest of things can go a long way! Write your partner a quick note, give them a foot rub, hold hands as you walk, pick up their favorite dessert, etc. The little things really add up over time. It shows your partner that you care for them and that you are happy you are together.

Clear the air

Avoid waiting till you are both fighting to bring up grievances. This only makes them become blown out of proportion. Make it a priority about once a week to ask your spouse if there is anything you have done to cause distance between you. It's important that both parties in a marriage know that they are interested in one another's feelings, even if they may cause an upset.

Throw away the score sheet

Many couples are not aware of it, but they unconsciously keep score of who does more chores, who get to hang out with their friends more, who has more money, who has more free time, etc. The sad thing is, couples tend to silently allow the resentment from these tallies to build up, which then negatively impacts many aspects of the marriage. Marriage is a team sport, if someone *is* winning, you are both losing. Throw out that silent score sheet and mentally keep shredding it till it becomes a habit *not* to keep score.

Apologize already

"I'm sorry" tends to be a heck of a lot harder to say than "I love you." No one likes admitting when they are in the wrong and at times, an apology can feel a lot like an admittance of defeat. No one is able to be right all the time. Your relationship with your spouse is much more important than being right. If you realize that the fight you are having is stupid and doesn't play a role in the bigger picture of things, learn to suck up your pride and say you are sorry. Your marriage should mean more to you than winning an argument.

Respect your spouse's time

There are many times that you ask your spouse to do something and months go by without lifting a finger to do it. Resentment builds drastically, which is no fun for either party. Instead, practice asking for what you want at a time that your spouse is able to do it for you. Asking for them to do things at more opportune times aids in a successful marriage because it shows them that you respect their time and are paying attention to their wants and needs as well.

Change the way your spouse sees you

In a marriage, you and your spouse are going to see many sides of one another. Human beings are naturally visual creatures. While this is part of sharing a life together, it can be quite helpful on occasion to portray yourself in a certain light. For instance, a woman could ask their husband to choose their lingerie before heading to bed. These little quirks help to tease one another, making them think about what their spouse is wearing *all* day so that they are anxious to come home.

Take initiative

Intimacy often times takes a backseat when it comes to living in the busy world the majority of us reside in today. But it is irresponsible for one or both spouses to wait for the other to make a move. Be spontaneous and give them a passionate kiss or bring home flowers and a delicious dessert. This will show your partner that you are physically, emotionally and mentally into them, even after all this time. Both of you will reap the rewards too!

Compare calendars

Check in with your partner each morning to see what is on their agenda for the day. This may seem very unromantic, but it helps to keep you both on the same page, even while you are apart. It also gives you the opportunity to check up on them later in the day, to encourage and support them. Everyone genuinely appreciates knowing that someone loves them enough to think about them during the course of their own busy days.

Pick connection over communication

Communication in 2018 happens largely over texting and email. Unfortunately, this provides couples with a lot of instant gratification, which can boil down conversations being boringly about daily tasks, scheduling, and other logistics. It can feel a lot like the trading of shifts. You should strive to put more connection in your communication by balancing your outbox. For each "to-do" reminder you send your spouse, make sure you also take the time to send a connecting text, such as a photo of a happy memory you share or something like, "You make me so happy!" You could even go as far as sending a slightly flirty note that builds their anticipation.

Learning the Act of Forgiveness

Many of us equate the act of forgiving with a warm feeling, but it is actually the opposite. Forgiveness, especially when it comes to someone you love, can be painful. While it may sound great as it comes out verbally, it makes people struggle with hypocrisy on the inside. It makes us become plagued with an abyss of resentment and bitterness and should not be viewed as a lip service.

Feelings that are left unchecked will find a way to become verbally, mentally, emotionally, and even physically murderous. Forgiveness is not about simply forgetting about an offense or choosing to inflict a price for the offense.

It can be challenging to forgive someone that you thought would never hurt you in the first place. But you must learn to forgive in order to keep the marriage you are part of alive. Forgiving and letting go of the past is a vital tool to a healthy marital relationship. It also plays an important part in keeping yourself healthy emotionally as well.

You are inevitably wasting you and your partner's time and energy if you hold on to anger, insensitivity, betrayals, annoyances, old hurts, and disappointments. The prolonged nursing of a perceived hurt will eventually turn into bitterness and a hate that is difficult to rid yourself of. In other words, a lack of forgiveness can wear you down, which in turn, wears out the marriage. Resentment will gain momentum over time and take chips out of your marriage's foundation.

How to Forgive Your Spouse

- Be patient with yourself, forgiveness takes time. No need to hurry the process along.

- Forgiving your spouse does not mean you condone their behavior that hurt you.

- Accept the fact that you may not know the reason for your partner's mistake and terrible behavior.

- Do not plan to seek out retribution or revenge of any kind. If you are always putting energy to get even with them, this is just extending the pain they have caused. Plus, it will not make you feel any better.

- Do not continuously throw the mistakes of your spouse at them later on. You should also not use their errors as ammunition against them in future arguments.

- When the images of hurt or betrayal come to mind, think of a place that calms your mind or do something that distracts you from dwelling on these negative thoughts.

- Make the decision to forgive your spouse consciously.

- Be receptive and open to the act of giving forgiveness.

Asking for Forgiveness from Your Spouse

- Make a verbal apology that comes from your heart. This will also include a plan of action that you should perform in order to make things right again.

- Be patient with the partner you hurt. Forgiveness takes time, and you should not dismiss how your spouse feels about the betrayal you caused or tell them to "get over it."

- Be open to making amends with your spouse.

- Accept the consequences of your actions that created the hurt.

- Make a commitment to not hurt your partner in the same way in the future again.

- Show true remorse for the pain you have caused your spouse.

Why Marriages *Need* Forgiveness

All close relationships in life rely on forgiveness to thrive. We are all human beings and no matter how hard we try, inevitably make mistakes from time to time. We all have bad and grumpy days, and we sometimes say things we do not mean. Everyone deserves to forgive and be forgiven. No matter how strong a marriage is, it cannot be sustained without forgiveness long term. Why you might find it challenging to forgive your spouse, it is crucial for you to do so if you want your marriage to move forward.

Restoring Broken Trust

All marriages will go through difficult times thanks to trust being broken. In fact, the core of many problems within marriages occurs because of a breach of trust. The strength of marital relations requires a strong and trusting bond, which is why it is so vital to rebuild it when it does become damaged. If you find that your marriage is suffering from a lack of trust, this chapter is a must-read.

Take responsibility over your actions

If you are the one that is responsible for breaking the trust in your marriage, own your actions and apologize for them. Taking responsibility if the first step to seek out forgiveness and state your commitment to do whatever you have to in order to restore it.

If you are the one that must offer forgiveness, do not make excuses for your spouse's behavior, but be willing to take responsibility for any actions that you did that might have contributed to the breakdown of your relationship. Remember that forgiving does not instantly fix everything.

Forgiveness might occur quickly, but trust is restored slowly

Trust and forgiveness are two wildly different things. When you are wronged by your partner, you should learn to forgive them as quickly as possible. On the other hand, you should give your trust gradually over time. Forgiveness can be given, but trust can only be earned. Forgiveness is the first step in paving the way to restoring trust.

Do not retaliate

It is natural when you have been wronged by anyone to feel the urge to punish the person who hurt you. But you should do your best to fight the temptation to use their offenses as ammunition in the future. Do not constantly hold negative things over your spouse's head. While you may want them to feel the pain that they have caused you, it only is damaging the trust between the two of you even more. Holding grudges is like drinking poison and hoping that the other person dies. Discuss clear guidelines to how you want the trust to be restored, but you should never punish the other person for making a mistake.

Consistency is key

While you and your partner are undergoing the process of rebuilding trust, you both must do your best to be consistent in both what you say *and* do. This is an important part of bringing security. There are sadly no shortcuts to restoring the trust that has been lost.

Be willing to give up some freedoms temporarily

Just like when you break your arm, it must be put into a cast in order to restrict movement to allow it time to heal. The same goes for broken trust in that you both must be willing to give up freedoms and accept restrictions to allow the time you both need to mend. This can be pretty uncomfortable, but it is crucial. Both parties should be willing to put away their pride to do whatever necessary to rebuild trust. This may mean putting a filter on your electronic devices, putting a tracking app on your phones, giving yourselves a curfew, or anything else that provides reassurances to one another.

No secrets

Secrets are as dangerous as lying in marriages. Secrecy is the ultimate enemy of intimacy. When you get married, you must be willing to provide one another a master key to one another's lives. Don't have a conversation with your spouse that you don't want them to hear, don't look at websites you wouldn't want them to see or go somewhere you don't want them knowing about. Transparency is crucial to trust building.

Surround yourself with positive influences

If you constantly hang out with people that are untrustworthy, it is understandable if your partner finds it harder to trust you and your judgment. Learn to be intentional about the people you choose to hang out with, especially when you are married. Choose to spend your time outside of your marriage with a small and trusted group of individuals who do not tempt you to act upon things that could further hurt your relationship.

Refuse to fall back into the same behavior

When there has been a breach of trust in specific areas, it can be easier for the spouse who was wronged to think that their partner might be a repeat offender. As human beings, we are all a work in progress, but you must realize that when you make bad decisions in repeated negative areas, you reopen old wounds, which makes it much more difficult to rebuild trust. Do everything you can to not fall into a vicious cycle of empty apologies and making empty promises. Take initiative to change your overall behavior in order to improve your marriage.

Keep moving forward

A big part of the reason why many marriages do not last is that one or both partners give up when the going gets rough. You must commit to love one another no matter what life brings the two of you. Do not lose hope, no matter how much your marriage might be struggling.

Getting Over the Past to Rekindle Your Marriage

One of the biggest desires married couples have is to stay together forever within a healthy, happy, and loving relationship. But holding on to past can hurt not only the wronged spouse but the entire marriage.

It is natural to feel betrayed and have a loss of trust in your partner when they hurt you. Once you have been hurt multiple times, your emotions can close up, and your heart can turn slightly to stone. This shuts down the ability to be close, both verbally and sexually. This means that your spouse becomes more of a roommate than an intimate partner.

To recapture the love that your marriage once had and to restore happiness, here are some steps to follow to get back to the way things were.

Identify the hurt

Step back in time to the first hurt and remember the way you reacted; did you brush it off, attempt to talk to your spouse or did you just shut down and cry? Did you feel understood and heard? Once you have reminisced about your first hurt, trace your steps back and see if the first hurt is similar to the others afterward. This will help you to clarify how you feel and provide you with a place to start to talk about your feelings with your spouse.

Sit down and talk

Invite your spouse to talk with you by letting them know that even though the first time they hurt you seemed small, it has grown bigger and you have since not let it go. By taking the time to acknowledge your feelings and letting them have a chance to take it seriously, you are giving yourself a first step to let go of the pain that haunts you, which enables you to move forward.

Listen

Make it a practice to take turns talking to one another. Have two monologues instead of a dialogue. Learn the importance of putting your feelings to the side to allow your partner to speak. Do not interrupt them and really attempt to step into their shoes. Then switch roles. This will give you both a chance to feel heard. You will hear even the smallest things differently when you choose to consciously listen, which allows the both of you to create a new perspective.

Be present and check in

Once you have listened to one another, you are now at the present time, which allows you to really think of the hurts you need to let go. Hurt usually stems directly from misunderstanding and miscommunication. Hurt makes us forget to check in with your spouse and hear them correctly. Checking in helps you to restore the trust with your partner. Talking to one another without blame can give you a chance to resolve painful feelings and not carry them with you to the future. This way you both have a much better chance of resolving those painful resentments and remain present at all times.

Create a plan to keep your marriage current

After you have discussed your hurts and worries with your spouse, you will both

feel understood and listened to. For the future, make an agreement to talk as soon as hurt happens. Don't allow hurt to stack on top of one another.

Prove that change has occurred

Often times, both spouses are responsible for hurting one another. This means that it is vital that both of you go out of your way to prove to one another that you have changed. This means acquiring the skill of patience. When you both have genuinely overcome your behavior, then patience is needed to change the attitude towards the healing process.

Patience is a virtue

The awakening to hurt from both parties can dredge up many negative feelings. When it comes to healing, it takes time to think about and process the things that have occurred. Through patience, your spouse will come to realize that making changes goes way beyond how they act towards you. You must also allow yourself time to heal from the past. It is a natural process that cannot be rushed.

Awareness

There will finally come a day that you realize that your spouse has grown from the consequences of their actions. Guards still remain up as the powers of observation are heightened. This allows both parties to regain the hope they need as they can see new things coming upon the horizon. Expected behaviors diminish, and new, more loving ones take their place. Respect and trust are allowed to grow rapidly. Do not rush this step, however, Let it grow and unravel as it does. Make sure you are still making observations that allow you to see the trust between you and your spouse grow.

Learning to Love Yourself Again

One of the hardest things to grasp about fixing marriages is the blatant fact that it initially begins with *you*. While some of the resentment and emptiness you feel may be partially your spouse's fault, much of it stems from your inner self. Self-abandonment instills the negative feelings that make resentment in the marriage grow. Dysfunctional marriages will continuously grow despite your efforts to patch things up with your spouse. In order to get down to the nitty-gritty of what might be ruining your marriage, it might be time to look at yourself in the mirror.

You might be abandoning yourself if you are:

- Making your partner feel responsible for how you feel
- Turning to addictions to numb negative feelings
- Judging yourself
- Ignoring how you feel by honing in on what is happening in your head rather than your body

Developing Self-Love in a Marriage

Learning to love yourself is a life-long and ongoing process. Even marriages that have a healthy amount of self-love could have more. Here is how to maintain self-love within your marriage!

Maintain independence and space

You should never allow your marriage to absorb your entire identity. You should never find yourself losing your entire self-worth and what makes you, you. In order to keep your marriage healthy, you need to keep your own friends, interests, and rituals. Spend a healthy allotment of time doing the things that you find to nurture your soul.

You are the master of your happiness

No matter how hard they try, your spouse cannot make you happy. You are the only one that is solely in charge of your happiness. It is not anyone else's responsibility but your own. If you rely on your spouse for contentment, you will literally drain the space that is between you.

Self-love is a habit you must be willing to practice over time. You must learn to adopt the mindset that happiness is a choice you make, which will then give you the power to cultivate happiness for yourself. This is much easier said than done, especially if you are one that allows your happiness to be dictated by others.

Choose to be present and don't just wait for the perfect moment to be happy. Quiet those negative thoughts and decide to be happy at the moment instead! Act on little things that make you happy by embracing the daily moments. Nurturing yourself by meditating or drinking a cup of tea will help to quiet the mind and allow you to be totally present at the moment and enjoy your days thoroughly.

You also need to make it a priority to work through the baggage from your past, for it is only then you will feel lighter, and it will be much easier to choose happiness. Working through pain is an ongoing process, but you should not let it hold you back from being yourself and finding contentment.

See yourself how your partner sees you

Those that are insecure strongly struggle to see what is good about themselves and are very dismissive of the things that their spouse sees in them. Ask your partner what they see in you and what they love about you. In fact, this can be a great and fun exercise for a date night. Write a list of 15-20 things that you love about one another and take turns reading them.

This will help you to internalize that you are an amazing person and truly believe it each day. The things that you are the most critical about are more than likely the pieces of you that your spouse thoroughly enjoys!

Don't become disheartened by your flaws

All people have flaws, it is what makes us who we are. But you need to recognize that relationships have a funny way of holding a mirror right up to those flaws. Things you have just learned to live with may irritate your spouse. While some flaws can easily be ignored, others need to be worked through. Do not be afraid to expose your flaws, for it is a natural part of a healthy relationship. Your flaws do not make you unlovable.

Forgive yourself

Holding grudges against yourself can majorly put a roadblock up against loving yourself. Do not beat yourself up over past actions.

Love is an action, not a feeling

Love is something that we consciously choose to do, not just something that we feel. While this is commonly said about choosing one another, it is something we forget when it comes to loving ourselves. Make it a priority to schedule "you time" each and every day. This is important, for you put yourself first, above any other priorities and commitments. Do something simple you enjoy! While one session at first will not make a huge difference, you will be surprised at how the creation of a self-love ritual will make a positive impact over time, and will provide great changes to your marriage as well!

Conclusion

Thank you for reading "

The next step is to take your time. If you need to, read this book again. You can read it as many times as you need to help you overcome things that may come up for you. Understand that once you heal the immediate trauma in your life, you are often presented with underlying traumas that you must now overcome. You may also face new traumas. We are often always working toward healing ourselves from something, in some way. This book is a great guide to help walk you through that healing process over and over again, as many times as you may need to.

Lastly, if you enjoyed this book and felt that it added value to your healing experience, please take the time to rate it on Amazon Kindle. Your honest feedback would be greatly appreciated.

Thank you.

www.ingramcontent.com/pod-product-compliance
Lightning Source LLC
Chambersburg PA
CBHW051744250726
48659CB00001B/239